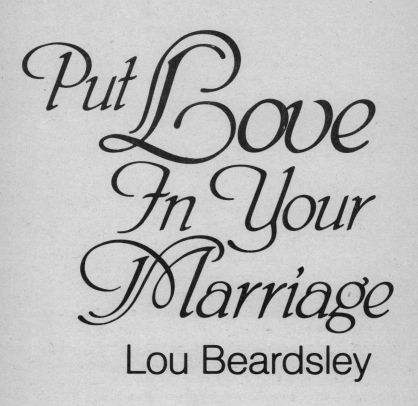

Put Love In Your Marriage

Lou Beardsley

Harvest House Publishers
Irvine, California 92714

Verses marked TLB are from THE LIVING BIBLE, copyright 1971, Tyndale House Publishers, Wheaton, Illinois, Used by permission.

Verses marked NASB are from the NEW AMERICAN STANDARD BIBLE, copyright The Lockman Foundation 1960, 1963, 1968, 1971, 1972, 1973, 1975 and are used by permission.

All verses marked RSV are from the REVISED STANDARD VERSION of the Bible, copyrighted © 1946, 1952, 1971, 1973. Used by permission.

All other scripture references are taken from the KING JAMES VERSION.

PUT LOVE IN YOUR MARRIAGE

Copyright © 1978 Harvest House Publishers, Irvine, California 92714
Library of Congress Catalog Card Number 78-55586
ISBN # 0-89081-122-9

To George,

my husband, best
friend and "life
companion."

Special thanks to my daughter, Nancy
Becknall and my friend, Toni Spry, for their
suggestions, notes and encouragement.

Contents

1

Happily Ever After

My husband and I stood on the rooftop of the large hotel watching the local disc-jockey-minister perform the wedding ceremony uniting two sophisticated city people. The glass windbreak protected us from the damp sea air and the skyscrapers peered down at the little gathering among the planter boxes full of blooming flowers. As the minister pronounced the couple husband and wife, he turned to pluck a daisy from a nearby flower box. "Love," he said, "is communicating with this flower!" A tall man in an embroidered gauze shirt that resembled a maternity smock whispered to us in hushed tones, *"Hea-vy!"* I kept my eyes averted from my husband, knowing I could never keep a straight face if I looked at him. I concentrated, instead, on the happy couple, beaming joyfully at each other without a thought of what the future might hold.

I reflected on the many weddings we've attended in the past few years. With all four of our children in their twenties, wedding invitations are even more frequent than letters urging us to enter *Reader's Digest* contests. We've been to weddings in cathedrals, to ceremonies in the redwoods, to those held in backyard gardens, in private homes, in little country churches, and now this one on the hotel rooftop.

Each marriage ceremony was unique, but all had one thing in common. The newlyweds started out their lives together in love, anticipating a fulfilled, happily-ever-after marriage. Now some of those couples have already divorced and others are having severe marital problems. There are those who have settled into the boredom of a marriage which is not all it could be; and some, who like several friends our own age, have struggled through twenty—even thirty—years together until their children were grown, and who are now choosing to go their separate ways.

More optimistically, however, there are couples who are experiencing God's best in their marriages. They are more in love today than when they were married. They aren't dissatisfied and disenchanted with their marriage partner, but are excited to be spending their time together. They are lovers—best friends—confidantes and *communicators*. This is not to say that there aren't disagreements and frustrations, but with problems come the excitement of learning the lessons God has to teach them in the difficult times. Each problem becomes a step to a new level of joy in each other. Do these couples have something others do not possess? Not really—except honest and open communication. They share each others joys, disappointments, hopes and dreams. They *listen* to each other, and not with just one ear and a distracted mind! They are listening to more than actual words as they tune into the feeling tones of their mate. They listen not only with their ears, but with their hearts.

When the minister at the rooftop wedding spoke of communicating with the flower, I couldn't help but think how much more important it would be for the young couple to learn to communicate with each other in a way that would carry them throughout their married life. Communication is the lifeblood of a marriage; without it, the relationship becomes terminally ill and eventually dies. Divorce is so prevalent today that proceedings can even be initiated by mail order! Things are so bad that we might not be surprised to find the next item on the consumer's market to be a sale catalog from which a person can order the specific type of divorce he needs in the off-season to save money! The fact remains that most divorces occur because somewhere along the line, communication has broken down between marriage partners and life has become boring and meaningless.

The Three "P's"

Is there an answer? Is there hope for those couples who would be willing to try to save their marriages, but who presently find they are unable to really talk to each other about their deep needs?

I believe it is possible because I have seen marriages mended and love restored to an even greater degree than the couples ever dreamed possible. When a couple, especially the wife, determines that a change in attitude is in order, the first step toward resolving the difficulties has been taken. It isn't an "instant cure" and it takes the "three P's" to pull it off: Prayer, Persistence and Patience!

Prayer involves not only praying, but turning your marital problems over to God; and following His leading. Search for God's wisdom, through reading the Bible daily, and then attempt to apply His principles in living.

Persistence is refusing to give up even when we can't see results. It is continuing firmly and steadily on our chosen course—changing our attitude toward our spouse.

Patience is waiting calmly for the change you pray will occur, and having the faith that God is able to accomplish His will in His own perfect timing.

Breakdown of communication may have taken years to come to the point of qualifying your marriage for the "intensive care unit," so please remind yourself that your marriage problems and injured feelings aren't going to heal in a day. The important thing, in turning an ailing marriage around, is practicing the right kind of medicine—a change in attitude. Pessimism must become optimism; silence, enthusiastic interest. Nagging must change to admiring; antagonism to acceptance; rigidity to flexibility;

and a low self-image to feelings of adequate self-worth. Our attitude is so important and *so* visible! We convey our feelings to others by our attitude, even without words.

Mirror, Mirror on the Wall

If we gals are going to be the ones initiating the change of attitude, where do we begin?

How about our self-image? Psychologists tell us that until we can accept ourselves, we don't have the capacity to love and accept others. My self-image could stand improving—how about yours? Most of us have features, character traits, personality hang-ups, physical or mental limitations which we would like to change.

If our particular hang-up is physical or something that *can* be changed, I'd say, "Go to it!" (If it's medically safe and you can afford it, it will undoubtedly give you self-confidence that you now lack.) If your self-image can be bolstered by donning contact lenses, joining weight watchers, undergoing cosmetic surgery for a nose-job, or visiting the orthodontist to correct those crooked teeth that cause you to adopt that "closed lip" smile for family photos —then don't put it off!

If, however, your undesired trait or physical attribute, etc. is something you can't change, you have but one course of action: accept it! God created each of us uniquely to fit the purpose in life which He has for us, and *God does not make mistakes!*

Reading Psalm 139 we know that God saw us

being formed in our mother's womb and that He knew exactly what we would be like. If we have let ourselves get fat or messy or grouchy, that's *our* fault and we can do something about it. But for those features we cannot change, we must thank God that He has a special design for us and accept ourselves. Remember, we are much more critical of our own looks than anyone else. Think of the least attractive friend you have and ask yourself if you like her less because she has a big nose, is six feet tall and is covered with freckles? Of course, you don't—you love her just as she is, and you don't even notice her outward appearance because of her inner beauty. What we *are* speaks louder than how we look.

A person with a good self-image is one who thinks of others first because she knows who she is, where she's going, and is confident that she is a God-created "original" being. She naturally impresses people as being outgoing and loving because she is interested in us.

Ask God to help you to accept yourself, just as you are (when you have made such changes as are possible), and to make you sensitive to the needs of others. As you listen to other people and empathize with them, they will nearly always respond positively to you. Their responses will, in turn, give you a renewed sense of self-worth.

When you apply these principles to your own husband (and marriage), he will begin to see "the new you" and there may be some exciting surprises in store for you. Accepting yourself helps you to be able to accept your husband, "warts and all." God created him, too, and He can make any changes necessary to mold your husband into the kind of man He intended him to be. The only help God needs from you is your cooperation in leaving the remodeling to Him while you search your own heart for changes in attitude that need to be made. Your new, loving attitudes will be the bridge to rejuvenated communication with your mate. It could take a week, several months, or more than a year; and that's where the "three P's" are important — prayer, persistence and patience.

Our Way or the Good Way?

We have the promise in the Bible that if any two of us agree on earth concerning anything we ask for, God will do it for us. That's a powerful statement, but Jesus made it and He meant it. The hard part comes as we wait for His perfect timing! We know from Isaiah 55:8, 9 that God's ways are not our ways.

In his book, *Praying Jesus' Way*, Curtis Mitchell — a professor and popular conference speaker from Biola College — says that we can see God's ways are not our ways when we read how He chose to conquer Jericho by having the Israelites march around the city blowing horns until the wall fell down. That's hardly what a modern military strategist would consider doing, is it? There was Gideon and his little band of men marching down the hill, carrying torches and breaking glass pitchers while blowing horns to scare the enemy. (You may recall that they scared them so badly the enemy got confused and began fighting each other!)

If you wanted to teach one of your children a lesson, you wouldn't have him get swallowed by a big fish and "barfed up" on the beach three days later. God's mind simply doesn't run in the same vein as ours. So, though it's God's will that our marriage be healed, the timing and method will be His, not ours.

God says, "First take the log out of your own eye, and then you will see clearly to take the speck out of your brother's eye (Matthew 7:5 NASB.) That's why it's going to take His timing to accomplish this miracle of a mended marriage. But think ahead to that great day when the wall between you and your husband comes tumbling down. That will help you to sustain the needed patience.

A true, dramatic change of heart usually produces speedy results, and it is dependent upon your willingness to try to follow the concepts and suggestions given in this book. I can't guarantee a 100 percent cure because many factors are involved in a communication breakdown, and everyone's marriage is different. However, I can say that any ideas presented here, to help build stronger bridges between marriage partners, have worked in thousands of cases. I pray yours will be one of those.

2

Setting the Stage

When a play or movie is being presented, the stage set plays an important part in communicating the message. The drama wouldn't be nearly so effective if portrayed against a plain wall and no props. We'd have to imagine the setting.

The same principle holds true when it comes to communicating with our husbands. The setting is vital. We've all heard the old adage, "The way to a man's heart is through his stomach." Yet, how many of us recognize that the dinner hour can set the stage for the entire evening? The atmosphere, the food, the table setting, the conversation—all contribute their part to a restful, communicative evening or one where our husband escapes to the TV, behind a newspaper or goes out with the boys.

The atmosphere of a home does not depend upon its current market value, its furnishings or whether you regularly serve steak or tuna casserole. It is dependent, for the most part, upon the woman of the house. A home can be very modest, yet be comfortable, neat, attractive and possess a warm atmosphere. It may require more effort on the part of the wife to accomplish this, but when a little extra work is weighed against the burden of a permanent lack of communication with your husband, it's a small price to pay. If you think the extra laundry, making yourself attractive and clean before your husband arrives home and sacrificing instant meals for those which require more preparation is too much trouble, let me tell you of my close friend, Nell Chinchen, a missionary in Liberia.

"Something Special"

The first several years Nell and her husband, Jack, spent in Africa, they were deep in the bush country, living in a bamboo house. In their early 40s, Nell and Jack had the four youngest of their seven children with them—a junior high daughter, twin sons who were eight years old and their youngest daughter who was a pre-schooler. Nell spent several hours each day working in the health clinic. She also led Bible classes for women and teenagers, was midwife for their village, taught her own children their school lessons, entertained visitors at the mission station and supervised the running of her household.

This past summer, Nell and Jack were home on furlough and my husband and I joined them for an outdoor barbecue. As we were setting the picnic tables, I glanced over and saw Nell placing salad forks next to the dinner forks.

"Salad forks for a picnic?" I asked her.

"You should have seen how we lived in the bush!" she laughingly replied. "Every night we dressed for dinner, had cloth table linens and napkins, candlelight and china! People who came over from the States said they'd never seen anything like it."

Later, as I pondered the reasons for Nell's elaborate dinner preparations for the seemingly "wild bush country," I came to realize her motivation. She was teaching her children a valuable lesson. She was creating an atmosphere for her husband and family at dinner time that would mentally transform their little bamboo house, in the middle of the jungle, into an elegant home in the suburbs.

It would have been easy for Nell to "let it all hang out" in the humid tropics—with no ice, boiled drinking water, bugs, lack of modern conveniences, little variety in their food and just plain physical exhaustion. Mealtimes could have become overly casual, with manners almost nonexistent; and with the eating habit serving only to replenish the body. But this was not to be the case. This ambitious wife and mother took the time and effort to make their dinner hours special. Through sharing, communicating, and joyfully loving—their evening meal was something which they all looked forward to. They were not only refreshed in body, but in spirit as well. Should we, with all our modern conveniences, do any less?

You Don't Say?

In order to be sure our husbands don't feel they are being manipulated, it is best for us to give forewarning before dramatically changing our mealtime routine. We should let them know that we realize our dinner hour has been a little on the undesirable side, for some time now, and that we are about to turn over a new leaf.

There are three ways in which we can bring about a change in our setting. We need to have positive actions, positive attitudes and a positive atmosphere.[1] By changing our actions, our attitude becomes in tune with them, thereby providing the changed atmosphere.

What you *don't* say often conveys more than what you *do* say. In Norm Wright's book on family communication, he speaks of verbal and nonverbal behavior. If we are being honest, our verbal and nonverbal communication will match. There are many phrases we can use which, by the tone of voice, can be either complimentary or slurring. A simple, "Yes, dear" can be either respectful and loving or (when uttered in a sarcastic tone) very caustic.

Below is a chart showing nonverbal gestures and their "results." See how your nonverbal cues match up with your verbal communication.

1. Norman Wright, *An Answer to Family Communication* (Irvine, CA: Harvest House Publishers, 1977), p. 35.

NONVERBAL CUE	RESULT: WARMTH	RESULT: COLDNESS
Tone of voice	soft	hard
Facial expression	smiling, interested	poker-faced, frowning
Posture	leaned toward other person, relaxed	leaned away from other person, tense
Eye contact	look into the other person's eyes	avoid eye contact
Touching	touch each other softly	avoid touching
Gestures	open, welcoming	closed, guarding oneself, keeping the other person away
Spatial distance	close	distant

As you can see from these nonverbal cues, it is possible to say things that are nice to hear, and yet contradict our very words by our actions. That is why our actions and attitudes must reflect the loveliness of our speech.

The Props

A little extra effort in obtaining the props for the stage set will enhance our new atmosphere at dinner time. To establish the idea of warmth and comfort, we need visual aids. Buy some inexpensive no-iron table cloths and napkins. Put them on the table each night at dinner, along with some kind of centerpiece. Strawflowers in a bean pot, flowers from your garden in a mason jar, an African violet in a ceramic pot, a bowl of fruit—use anything that looks festive. Candles, especially the scented ones, add a romantic touch; but, if your husband hates eating by candlelight, I'd suggest waiting to use candles until summer when it's not dark at dinner time. Hopefully, by the next winter, he will be so used to the candlelit dinners that he will enjoy them.

Put some mellow records on the stereo or turn the radio to a station which features relaxing music.

Make a special effort to have a tasty meal that is well-balanced. There are hundreds of good cookbooks that have simple menus if you are just learning.

Keep the conversation on a positive key and speak softly and lovingly. If your husband criticizes your dinner, he may just be extra tired and grumpy, so agree with him. Tell him that next time you'll try to do better. Don't be disappointed and take his criticisms personally; remember, this is a new way of living and it may take a few evenings for him to appreciate what you are seeking to accomplish. Do everything you can to please your mate. Pray. And let God do the rest!

One good idea is to start off dinner conversation by having the children tell about the funniest thing that happened to them that day, and then add something of your own. Don't bring up anything unpleasant; and if the children begin to argue, excuse them from the table lovingly, but firmly, to be dealt with later. If you explain to your youngsters beforehand that you want to make dinnertime an extra special treat for Daddy, they will likely think of it as a game and do their best to cooperate. If the children are older, you can share with them how you feel the dinner hour should be mentally, physically and spiritually uplifting, and ask them to help you to make it that way.

If you have no children at home, it will be easier to have a serene atmosphere at the table. Make sure you are dressed attractively, have showered and put on makeup. In short, look your best. Steer the conversation to whatever your husband's interests are and simply listen to him, with an occasional encouraging comment. If he wants to tell you about last Saturday's golf game, praise the Lord! That's a beginning to communication.

Be sure to get "prayed up" before evening. Ask God to give you the proper attitude and to keep you from responding negatively to anything your husband may do or say. When an evening starts out well, it more often than not continues in this vein. If the dinner hour is unpleasant, the hours that follow have to be extra special to turn the tide.

Prepare as much of your dinner ahead, as you are able, in order to be relaxed when your husband sits down to dinner. If you've been rushing and frustrated while preparing the food, that's the kind of atmosphere which will prevail at dinner and throughout the evening. If you work, do as much food preparation ahead of time as you can—either the previous evening or before you leave home in the morning. If necessary, precook foods on the weekend and freeze them ahead, or use a slow cooker to cut down on your preparation time.

Don't give up if this doesn't seem to be working out the way you'd hoped. The whole family will gain by your efforts in the long run, including yourself. It's better for your digestion and health and you will come to appreciate the serene dinner hour so much you wouldn't want to go back to the old way.

Backstage in the Bedroom

Setting the stage for the dinner hour is very important, but so is atmosphere in the bedroom. If your husband is happy with the sexual aspect of your marriage, usually he is happy with the other facets and your communication is good. If there is a problem in a couple's sexual relationship, more often than not it extends to other areas of the marriage, and communication is one of the first to suffer.

God invented sex for both husband and wife to enjoy and *only* within the confines of marriage. Somehow, through the years, various old wives' tales got started that sex was only for men's enjoyment and that women were simply "the victims" of their husbands' animalistic behavior. In counteracting these distorted views, society rushed to the opposite end of the pendulum and the result is sexual promiscuity, "open" marriages, live-together-arrangements, and the immorality so common today.

If you have a problem in the area of sex, are a newlywed, or a "veteran" of years of wedded bliss, one of the best books written on the subject is *The Marriage Act*, by Tim and Beverly LaHaye. The book approaches marital sex from a

Christian standpoint, and is written in good taste. Women, you'll find the books *The Fulfilled Woman* (by Toni Spry and me) and *The Total Woman* (by Marabel Morgan) beneficial. Written by Christian women, both texts contain helpful information.

The best advice I can offer for approaching a problem in the area of sex is to pray for the right attitude. If you find yourself resenting having to participate in lovemaking, recognize that this feeling does not come from God. Those physical needs were placed within your husband by Him and you have them, too, whether or not you realize it!

When you pray in faith for anything—whether it is an attitude or something more tangible— you need to be aware of one thing: God "gives us our ticket when we board the train." When the exact moment of need arrives, that is when the prayer is answered, not before.

When the children of Israel escaped to the Red Sea, when pursued by the Egyptians, they discovered the sea was not parted and waiting for them to cross. The waters didn't separate until the Egyptians were in sight and it was time to go.

When you pray for the right attitude toward sex, don't expect to get up in the morning with an eager anticipation of that evening which will continue to grow and build all day until you're feeling very romantic by the time your husband gets home. Do the necessary things to provide the correct atmosphere in your bedroom—clean sheets (sprayed with cologne), shining furniture, a scented candle, a pretty nightgown, soft music, indirect lighting (preferably one small lamp burning), and *you*—smelling clean and fresh. As you climb into bed and your husband takes you in his arms, *then* the change of attitude comes. Expect it. Trust God for it. And it will be there when you need it!

If your husband is a Christian and you have an unsatisfactory sex life, pray about it together. God will always honor those prayers. Perhaps you don't know if your husband is happy with the sexual aspect of your marriage. One good way to find out is to ask him. Don't, however, dissolve in tears if he registers some complaints. Be thankful that he is open enough to tell you rather than confiding in another woman. Thank him, and promise that with the Lord's help, you will aim to improve and do just that. When a man's physical needs are met, both from the standpoint of good food and fulfilled sex, he is much more likely to be communicative with you in all other areas of your marriage, too.

3

Barriers to Communicating

Fear

Remember when you were in high school and everyone had to recite in front of the class? Maybe it was a book report or a speech. The very thought of it made your stomach tie up in knots and you dreaded it from the time the assignment was given. When the awful day came, your palms were sweaty, your mouth dry, and your feet felt like two bags of cement as you walked to the front of the room. Your voice sounded crackly and you either stuttered, spoke too fast or giggled with nervousness between each sentence. There were those few people, however, who actually seemed to enjoy it. They walked self-confidently to the front of the class, spoke in a clear voice, threw in a little humor, and proceeded to entertain you.

What made the difference between these born communicators — as they beamed with assurance and pulled down an ''A'' on their speeches — and the rest of the faltering, stammering members of the class? Fear! They simply were not afraid. They were enjoying themselves so much and were so interested in what they were telling you and your subsequent reaction, they forgot about themselves. It takes a natural extrovert to enjoy speaking to a group. Most of them are just as comfortable in a one-to-one situation and they rarely have a problem communicating in marriage. The introvert, however, finds it almost as traumatic being openly communicative with his mate as speaking to a group of people.

It is said that the way to conquer fear is to face it. Let's explore the various causes of fear, and possible solutions which will lead to the elimination of fear and improved communication with our mate and others. As you read, you will probably see yourself in one or more of these categories and, if you do identify with a particular type of fear, you can apply the principles of the solution to your own life and begin to overcome those fears which have hampered your communion with your husband or wife.

1. Fear of being rejected or hurt

Perhaps at some time during the courtship or early marriage relationship a thoughtless remark wounded the sensitive partner. He or she retired into his own shell, determined to protect his pride by not confiding anything really important. Whenever we hold back on communicating with our mate, it sooner or later becomes evident to him. When he realizes that we are not being open with him, he assumes the same position with us—he buries his innermost thoughts and feelings deep inside and the barrier goes up.

True love always carries a risk with it, on a human level. If we are to be honest and open and give of ourselves, we risk the possibility of being hurt. We are imperfect beings—so are our mates—and, eventually, we are going to hurt each other, either inadvertently or purposely.

What does the Bible say about the fear of being hurt? "God has not given us a spirit of fear, but of power and of love and of a sound mind." (2 Timothy 1:7) It also says that God binds the wounds of the brokenhearted, (see Psalm 147:3), so we won't be permanently disabled by crushed feelings. Our problems come from expecting too much of our mates. No one except God is completely dependable and our world needn't fall apart when our partner lets us down in one instance. There will undoubtedly be times when we let him down, too. Don't think of it as rejection—think of it as human failing. Then forgive and forget.

2. Fear Resulting from Background

Many of us come from families who trained us to keep our problems to ourselves and never share our feelings with anyone else. It was looked upon as a sign of weakness to admit that there were things in our lives which we could not handle. We have known many Christians who went through real times of trial without the benefit of intercessory prayer by fellow believers because they were too inhibited or too proud to ask for it. Their hesitancy to open themselves to close friends deprived them of the wise counsel they so desperately needed.

Often this is a problem between a married couple. Pride on the part of one or the other keeps them from admitting there is a problem until it becomes of such a serious nature they are forced to seek counseling. We need to overcome the burden of incorrect training. God tells us, "Bear . . . one another's burdens, and so fulfill the law of Christ" (Galatians 6:2).

3. Naturally reserved personality and temperament.

There are those persons whose personalities make it diffucult to share. They may be from families who were very open and loving; yet, they keep their problems to themselves. Often their noncommunication stems from a simple desire to spare their mates from worry. Or, it could result from a natural reticence, coupled with the idea that the problem isn't worth bothering about or that it could be embarrassing.

One very fine man shared in his Sunday School class that he had hesitated to ask for prayer for a situation in their family because they felt it would make them appear less "spiritual" than they felt their image to be. Only when the problem grew very grave was he able to speak of it. This man later told the class of feeling such a relief after sharing his burden with them. By opening up, allowing himself to be vulnerable, he experienced a new freedom and joy with his Christian friends.

In a marriage situation, particularly with newlyweds, this could also be the case. We are usually trying so hard to impress our loved one, we hate to admit we don't have it "all together." Not only do we deprive ourselves of the joy and closeness of shared confidences, we may be discouraging our mate from opening up to us. In 2 Corinthians 5:17 we are told that we are new persons in Christ. The old reserved personality must go! Jesus was a great communicator—the best who ever lived—and since He is living His life in us, through His Holy Spirit, we can be great communicators, too.

4. Lack of Self-Acceptance

We discussed self-acceptance in detail in chapter one, and if we do what we can with what we've got to work with, we can expect others to accept us as we consider how much God loves us and what He did for us. Do you realize that Christ would have come and died for you if you had been the *only* person on earth? Don't ever doubt your self-worth—God loves us all equally and has a special, wonderful plan for each of our lives.

5. Lack of Trust in God

Normally, a poor devotional life is the reason

for doubts and fears in being open with our mates. A limited knowledge of the Bible can cause us to doubt God. It's almost impossible to completely trust someone with whom you have only a nodding acquaintance. If you are unfamiliar with the Bible, your knowledge of God is limited. Jesus said, "Take my yoke upon you, and learn from me; for I am gentle and lowly in heart, and you will find rest for your souls" (Matthew 11:29 RSV). The more we learn of Him, the more we are able to trust Him and the more self-confident we become.

When we realize that God is in control of every situation, we can give Him our fears and doubts and worries with perfect assurance that He is able to handle them. When we are unable to trust God, we are unable to trust our marriage partner. Our recognition that God is completely trustworthy helps us to realize that He is also in control of our marriage. If He allows us to be in a particular situation, it is because that is His best for us. The Bible is full of good advice for every situation and only through familiarity with it, in our daily devotions, can we find the answers to our problems. Since we are told in the Scriptures to share with one another, we can open ourselves up with assurance to our partner, trusting God to take care of the outcome.

It is extremely important that we care enough to confront our mates with any problem that might arise and that we be completely honest and truthful. Nothing breeds distrust like being caught in a lie—even if it's just a "little white lie.'' It is very difficult to trust someone on whose word we cannot depend and lying is simply a form of self-protection.

Another thing we must remember: It is next to impossible to tell just *one* lie. That one nearly always needs another to cover for it, and the burden of guilt becomes intolerable as we pile one lie on top of another. The truth is so much easier, in the long run, and once it is confessed and the apology made, our consciences are clear. Marriage cannot survive without honesty and trust, and it is impossible to communicate openly while covering a web of lies. If we hold these unexpressed fears or concerns inside, they are bound to crop up some way. It is like holding a large beach ball under water. The pressure becomes so great we are eventually forced to let go, and up it pops to the surface!

6. Fear of Admitting We're Wrong

The reason young children have such a hard time getting along is because they hate so much to admit they are wrong. Somehow, the ego demands to be ''right.'' Even grown people will make excuses, lie, argue, become angry or even violent to try to prove that they are not in error. Not long ago, two friends were arguing over the location of a certain street in our city. One got out the map to prove his point only to have his friend insist that the map was wrong. Too many of us feel that others will lose respect for us if we admit we have made a mistake.

Many a minister or Bible teacher discourages his flock from bringing their problems to him because they feel he is always "on top of things." I remember one particular lady Bible teacher who was spiritual to the point of being smug. She discouraged the rest of us by appearing *never* to have a problem. We got the idea that we must have been doing something wrong, or God was somehow punishing us, because we seemed to encounter many problems in our own lives. Later, we found that this Bible study leader had a very serious family problem which she refused to share because she was afraid of losing her effectiveness as a teacher. However, not too long after this, the Lord removed her from her position because people were beginning to put her on a pedestal, thinking that she handled everything in her life perfectly.

It has been my experience, in teaching women, that they are very appreciative of my sharing my problems as well as my joys: my defeats as well as my victories. They can identify and they don't put me on a pedestal or feel defeated when things go wrong in their homes. Admitting that we often "blow it" is a sign of strength, not weakness, and draws us even closer to others. This is why it is so important to confess to our marriage partner that we have made an error. It encourages him to be honest with us even when he is wrong and gives us an opportunity to be loving and forgiving.

Whenever we are unable to communicate with

our mates because of fear, we *know* this is not God's will. When I feel afraid, I realize this is an attack from the devil and I repeat the Scripture, "Greater is He that is in me than he who is in the world" (see I John 4:4). I add, "Be gone, Satan, in the name of Jesus!" and the fear goes away with his departure. Don't live a defeated life because of fear or allow it to stand in the way of communicating with your husband.

4

The Communication Gap

Now that we are on our way to building a bridge across the communication gap in our marriage, what are the attitudes which need to be changed? This involves an honest searching of the heart and a teachable spirit. We need to ask ourselves, as we go through these examples of attitudes which causes communication breakdown, which ones apply to our lives. I can see several on which I need to concentrate. Let's pray that God will reveal to us those areas where our attitudes toward our husbands are displeasing to Him.

The Unbelieving Husband

Christian wives may make non-Christian husbands feel inferior.

The most frequently encountered problem I've found, in speaking to and with women, is that of the husband who is antagonistic toward spiritual things. How does a wife cope with a man who wants no part of Christianity? First, she must remember that it is the job of the Holy

Spirit to convict him of his spiritual needs. Leave the whole matter to God. We know what a temptation it is to point out to our husbands their lack of enthusiasm for church and their indulgence in activities which seem to us to be "un-Christian." But the Bible says "Win them, not with *words*, but by a gentle and quiet spirit" (1 Peter 3:1-4 TLB). There you are again—God's ways are not our ways!

Determine to leave the conversion or spiritual growth of your husband to God, pray for him, concentrate on his good points and begin to really listen to what he says from *his* point of view. Ask yourself, "Would I have agreed with him before I was a Christian?" If you answer this in the affirmative, don't blame him too much. Remember that you are the one who has changed. Try to understand him and be sympathetic and tolerant toward him even if you can't agree with him. Jesus did not agree with the way the woman at the well was living, but he was loving and forgiving toward her just the same.

A Fish Out Of Water

Consider what often happens when a woman becomes converted after marriage and her husband has not yet accepted the Lord. Her first impulse is to preach to him (he would call it nagging) and to get him to as many Christian functions as possible. At these affairs, he feels like an alien in a foreign land. Everyone speaks a certain "language." They use words and phrases like "fellowship," "witnessing," "born-again," and talk about something called "the rapture" which he doesn't even like to think about. People often seem intent upon getting him to fit into their mold. There are certain behavior standards which seem very strict to him regarding drinking alcoholic beverages, smoking, swearing and other activities which the world considers "normal." Many of these Christians attend church *twice* on Sundays, which seems weird to someone who is used to going only on Easter, Christmas and Mother's Day. There is also talk about giving large sums of money "to the Lord," and he feels he scarcely has enough to pay his bills, let alone give any away.

The husband's reaction to these Christians is predictable. He wants to see as little of them as possible because he is uncomfortable in their presence. What's worse, his wife seems to be making a subtle comparison between him and them, and *he* is coming out second best. She begins to nag him about becoming like them and changing himself. She doesn't respond to his overtures of affection as she did before. In fact, he begins to wonder if she still loves him at all. He is totally baffled by the situation. He sees only that he is exactly the same as he has always been, but that his wife has undergone an incredible change. She has become a "religious fanatic" and wants to drag him down the same road. He recognizes that it has driven a wedge between them and turned their satisfactory relationship into a frustrating one where he can never please her, and neither of them are happy.

When this type of behavior occurs in a home, some undoing must be done. An understanding of God's way of reaching an unbeliever is necessary, and His way is not one of critical rejection, but of total love and acceptance. The wife's position in this case should be to apologize for her wrong attitude, ask her husband's forgiveness, and then set about to change herself. By becoming more loving, more submissive, admiring her husband and—while being true to God's Word—following her husband's lead, she will (without a word) lead him to Christ.

We have this promise in 1 Peter 3:1, 2 TLB: "Wives, fit in with your husbands' plans; for then if they refuse to listen when you talk to them about the Lord, they will be won by your respect, pure behavior. Your godly lives will speak to them better than any words." It sounds like a tall order and if you can't conjure up the willingness to do it, ask God to help you to *be* willing to be *made* willing. We have seen this principle work over and over again.

The question is, how much do you want a Christ-centered marriage? There is only one way to have God's best and that is to be obedient to what He tells us to do. It may seem too hard, boring, humiliating and against all of our human reasoning; but, with faith that He is right, a sense of humor and a spirit of adventure, we can see our own lives and that of our husbands' transformed before our very eyes!

Learning To Listen

A woman went to her physician and said, "Doctor, I'm afraid that my husband has a terrible affliction. Sometimes I talk to him for hours and he literally does not hear a word I say!" The doctor replied, "Lady, that's not an affliction—it's a gift!"

Insensitivity is a problem with all of us, and in all relationships, but it is particularly acute with our husbands. We become "accustomed" to their faces, as the song goes, and scarcely notice their moods as we babble in their ear, absorbed with our own interests.

Often we've been home all day long, with only toddlers for company, and we're anxious for our husbands to come home so we can enjoy some adult conversation.

He, on the other hand, may have been talking for hours on end at work and longs for peace and quiet. As he walks wearily in the door and sinks into the nearest chair, we begin our "unloading" of the day's activities. "Junior fell down and got stitches in his chin . . . the washer is making a funny noise . . . one of our checks got lost in the mail and the next door neighbor's boy hit Susie again . . . " On and on and on we talk until he feels like rushing out the door and going back to work. Or, he makes his mind a blank and tunes us out.

Communication begins by listening. Sometimes we women get the idea that communication is *us* talking. Conversation is more than a continuous 90-minute monologue. It's not just "talking to hear yourself talk" (as my grandmother used to say, about *me*!). Communication is listening and making the right comments. It is being sensitive to the needs of our husband.

My husband is a whistler. When the day has been a good one, he comes up the front walk whistling a happy tune. When it has been frustrating or extra tiring, his whistler is silent. I've learned to listen for the sound of his day and set the atmosphere to meet his needs.

A stack of mellow records is soothing. An easy chair, his slippers, a hot or cool drink, according to the weather, are all relaxing. I always set the table first so that even if dinner isn't quite ready, it *looks* as though it is. Don't badger him with questions about what went wrong. Just be loving, gentle and cheerful. After dinner, when his stomach is full, you can ask him if there is anything he would care to discuss with you.

We need to make our husbands' homecomings special each night. We should be at least as glad to see him as the dog is! Tell him you appreciate how hard he works to support you, and see that your home is a place of refuge for him.

Listening is done with our hearts; talking is done with our mouths. As one pastor has said, we need to put our minds and hearts in gear before we set our mouths in motion. There's a delicate balance between "Sally Silent" and "Gloria Gabber." Many husbands don't open up and share because they know their wives aren't really listening. It hurts to have your innermost secrets fall on deaf ears.

Pray for sensitivity and listen for the nudging of the Holy Spirit when you're tempted to talk when you shouldn't. Don't allow listening to become a "lost art" in your home. I've found that when I listen to my husband, he will listen to me. This reflects the biblical principle, "Whatever you sow, you reap." (see Galatians 6:7).

Mrs. Buttinsky

"We interrupt this program to bring you a special news bulletin!" These words can make our hearts skip a beat. We expect to hear of some disaster or an announcement of national or worldwide significance. Our ears perk up and we listen carefully.

However, most interruptions do not bring this type of response. They cause, instead, a feeling of irritation directed toward the "interrupter." It means that he does not consider what we were saying to be as important as what he wants to say, or it indicates that he wasn't listening to what we were saying and could not wait for us to finish our sentence. I wish I could tell you I have this one licked — that I am always polite and never interrupt people. The fact is, I'm a compulsive talker and often I don't listen carefully to what people are saying, or else I think I know what they are going to say so I jump in with my opinion on it! It's a terrible habit, and one where I'm tripped up often.

Recently we visited a friend in the hospital who had just had surgery. We asked him about details of his illness. Imagine our surprise when, in the midst of his explanation, his dear wife took over and finished the story. She even contradicted him on some details only *he* could have known. My husband mentioned to me later that evening how rude he thought the wife was. I started to agree when I stopped short—I've been guilty of the same rudeness. This interrupting seems to be more common among women than men. One friend even told of a preacher whose wife chimed into the middle of his sermon to correct him. Small wonder he didn't retire from the ministry after that!

A helpful solution to this bad habit is to memorize Psalm 141:3 RSV. "Set a guard over my mouth, O Lord, keep watch over the door of my lips." We can pray that as we are tempted to interrupt our husbands, and God will shut the door of our lips so that we don't stifle our husbands' attempts to communicate with us. Many a man has retired behind a wall of silence because he never is able to finish a sentence anyway. Praise the Lord for my choleric husband who is not prone to silence. My interrupting only makes him irritated and he does not hesitate to remind me when I do it. If this is one of your faults and you have a quiet, retiring husband, this could be one of the main reasons for his silence. Repeating this Psalm is a great "lip-zipper," and be sure to apologize to your husband each time you interrupt him. If you keep your sense of humor, it could begin to take on the characteristics of a family joke and everyone in the household will become more careful about their "Pardon me, but's."

Build Him Up!

We, as wives, need to be loved, but our husbands need to be admired. If we don't give them the admiration they need, they tend to retire into a shell of reserve and silence. We deprive them of the thing they need most for self-acceptance and then wonder why they are not more outgoing. In the book, *The Fulfilled Woman*, Toni Spry and I devoted an entire section on how to successfully admire your husband, but the basic idea is as follows:

Give your husband to God, thanking Him for all his faults and asking that the Lord help you to accept your husband *just as he is!* Remember that his actions are probably a result of your attitude. Ask God to show you areas where you can sincerely admire your husband. Concentrate on his virtues and the reasons you married him in the first place. Is he a good father? A good provider? Handsome? Fun to be with? Intelligent? Athletic? Loving? Honest? Then, tell him how much you appreciate these qualities. Don't be self-righteous. Unless you have been the perfect wife with never a fault, don't expect perfection from your mate.

Begin by giving him a sincere compliment at least once every day for a week. You don't have to think up a new one each time, but rephrase it. If you particularly like something he is wearing, tell him, "I like those pants on you—they make you look very attractive." Or if he has a good feature, you might say, "I love your nose—it's really masculine." You could admire his strength as he moves something heavy. (Don't be sarcastic and tell him it takes real strength to heave his fat body out of the chair!) Tell him you are thankful that he loves his children so much, or that you are proud of his diligence in going to work every day. (Some men are chronic day-off-takers or job-hoppers).

One lady said to me, "When I tried complimenting my husband for the first time in 35 years," he said. "What's wrong with you?" so I stopped. If you find yourself in this lady's position, you probably need to tell your husband that you are sorry you've been so unappreciative, and that since God has shown you that you should change, you're going to tell him the things about him for which you are thankful. If he knows that you are sincere, he won't feel he is being manipulated.

Remember the nonverbal cues, and back up your compliments with action. You could cook his favorite dinner, surprise him with a new record or tape or some golf or tennis balls—just something to let him know you've been thinking of him. When I see an especially pretty greeting card, I buy it and sign it. Then I place it on the bureau in our bedroom where my husband unloads his pockets when he comes home from work. Sometimes cards can say things you find difficult to verbally express to him. Try this for one week and see if you can notice a difference in your husband's response to you. Hopefully, it will become a lifetime habit which will enrich your relationship.

5

Building More Bridges

In this chapter, we will continue to explore attitudes which need to be changed in order to bridge the communication gap between a wife and her husband.

Stimulating Conversation

It has been said that great minds talk about ideas; average minds talk about events; small minds talk about other people.

If your husband is a Christian, you have a wealth of information to share which is uplifting and exciting—concepts God is teaching you through His Word, small miracles He is doing in your life each day, thrilling events occuring among the Christian population, books you've been reading—all of which make for stimulating conversation.

If your husband is not a Christian, how about discussing world events? Read your daily newspaper or a magazine like *U.S. News and World Report* or *Time* or some other periodical which keeps you up on politics and important news. If he is a nonintellectual, bone up on whatever his main interest is so that you can discuss it with him. If he's a sports fan, ask God to give you an interest in football or whatever his favorite sport might be, and watch the game. I have become an Oakland Raider fan so I could share my husband's enthusiasm for the team. By the end of the season I knew most of the player's names even though I spent part of the games preparing snacks for my husband and sons, doing crewel embroidery and crocheting. You can learn a lot by just watching one quarter of play. (I must confess I learned quite a bit about football when our oldest son was a star halfback in high school; but it proves that where there is an incentive, it is possible for a woman to understand football. I still don't see most of the penalties, but at least I can appreciate a good pass or run and it makes my husband happy when I comment on it.) If your husband is a participator rather than a spectator, attend his games. Our daughter's mother-in-law takes along her knitting and watches her husband bowl every week. He appreciates her interest and it gives them an extra area of communication.

We wives realize that it is very difficult to get overly excited about things pertaining to electronics, carpentry, architecture, manufacturing, mechanics, bookkeeping, scientific data, engineering concepts, etc. We don't understand the intricacies of our husbands' work and it wouldn't be honest to pretend that we do. But, one solution is to ask questions! You will learn and he will enjoy explaining.

If he tells you about a problem at work, offer to pray about it. However, one thing we must remember: Do not worry about his problems, only *pray* about them. One husband told me that he had stopped sharing his concerns about business with his wife because she worried too much about them. Also, be careful not to carry a grudge against someone else because of what your husband tells you. Perhaps someone has offended your husband and you become angry with this individual. God will give your husband the grace to bear the offense, but that doesn't necessarily mean you've been automatically granted sufficient grace. You may find yourself carrying around the bitterness within yourself. I recall one lady who found it very hard to be civil upon meeting one of her husband's superiors because of some unkind actions this man had taken against her husband several years before. The man could detect the resentment in her attitude when they met and a good relationship between them was impossible, even though her husband had long forgotten the incident. Harboring this kind of bitterness can result in ulcers, colitis, hypertension and other physical ailments. If our husband tells of a wrong committed against him by another person, we need to trust God for the matter and pray for grace for our husband and a change of heart by the other person.

Vivé le Difference!

It is true that we women need to talk about our housework problems, so try adopting an older woman in your church or neighborhood if you don't have parents near by. It is difficult for husbands to get excited about putting together a new recipe (hopefully, he will get excited about eating it) or whether paper towels or newspapers are better for washing windows. Understanding the difference between men and women may help you to accept your husband's lack of attention to the little details of the home.

God has made man so that he sees things from a larger perspective than woman. Picture a very large square and in it several printed words: job, advancement, promotion, future plans, insurance policies, children's college, larger home, money for next year's vacation, Christmas plans, hospital insurance, etc. A large scope of interest involving the heavy responsibility of being a husband, father and provider—this is what God has given your husband. Now, picture a smaller square inside the large square. This one is you and me—wives. In our square are printed such words as: dinner menu tonight; take clothes out of dryer; help Susie with homework; shop for new dress; fertilize Creeping Charlies, etc. Details—small ones that will be forgotten shortly after we do them or make the decision. But that's our world and that's how God intended it. Frankly, I'm glad I have only the small details to care about—nothing earth-shaking or serious enough to mean the difference between security or poverty for my family! God made men and women different, and praise Him for the difference!

Who's Your Best Friend?

Everyone needs a special friend in whom she can confide and trust that her conversation will go no further. A friend who is a prayer partner, who will weep when we weep, rejoice when we rejoice—who knows all about us but loves us in spite of it—is invaluable. However, this friend should not take the place of our husbands. Our deepest needs and emotions were meant to be shared with him, not with another friend. If we depend upon a woman friend to meet this need in our lives, we will find ourselves turning more to the friend and less to our husband. As this happens, he will begin to commune less with us. Some day, when the children are grown and the friends have perhaps moved away, we will find ourself in the position of having only that man we married as a sharing partner. If no communication has been built up through the years, we're going to have a very frustrating, boring twilight of life.

Women who have been widowed tell us that the hardest part is the thought that the person who cared most about every facet of their lives is gone. Most husbands would literally die for their wives. They would risk their own lives to save their wives from a burning building or a sinking ship or a criminal. They care more for us than any other human being on earth. We need to draw closer to them—not use another friend as a wedge between us.

Two Against One

We must be very careful not to criticize our husbands to *anyone*, including our best friend. It is completely against God's will. The Bible says, "She who shames her husband is as rottenness to his bones." (see Proverb 12:4). Whenever anyone speaks to me of her "horrible" husband, I remind myself that there are two sides to every problem and tactfully change the subject. Another person's marriage is like the tip of the iceberg. We do not see the gigantic hidden portion; therefore, we are not in a position to judge from the little we know about it.

It is unfair to your friend to make her a sounding board for your complaints against your husband. God has not given her the grace to bear your trials so, more often than not, she carries around a negative attitude against your husband. This burden weighs upon her whenever she thinks about it and causes her to harbor bitterness against him. Then when you and your husband have patched up your differences, she finds it hard to forgive him and may even dislike him intensely.

On the other hand, many a strong-willed, well-meaning friend has persuaded her weaker sister to divorce her husband on the evidence of what she has been told. This can bring on an intolerable burden of guilt to the friend when she realizes what she has done, particularly if the woman who divorces her husband is sorry afterward. God knows the future, and He understands every aspect of your problem. This is why His advice is so sound. He knows the dire consequences that result from a woman criticizing her husband to a friend, and He is protecting us by His warning. If you find yourself over-involved with a friend, to the point where you are sharing too much about your marriage with her or are on the receiving end of her confidences, discuss the matter with her. Tell her you feel that both of you are wrong and turn over a new leaf together. Your friendship will be more uplifting as it takes on a positive aspect.

I've Got A Secret

Many a man has expressed chagrin that his wife has "spilled the beans" and shared something private with someone else. This can have drastic results in the case of a husband who is a pastor, doctor, lawyer, counselor or in secret government work where confidences cannot be violated. One woman had the awful experience of sharing something with a couple that her husband had told her in confidence, omitting any names, only to find that the very couple she was telling were the ones involved. That was the last time her husband shared anything of consequence with her.

We have a friend who has a top secret job with the Space program and he can't discuss his job with his wife at all. He can't even tell her where he is going when he leaves on a business trip. She is given a number, by his company, that she may call in an emergency and they will reach him for her. What little she does know concerning her husband's business, she keeps strictly to herself. And we should treat all our husband's confidences this way. Remember that whatever you tell your best friend will almost positively be talked over with her husband or another friend. Our husbands should be able to trust us to keep their secrets without divulging them to anyone else.

One man we know never shares anything but general information with his wife because, he says, if he does it's like putting it in the newspaper — it will be all over town by morning! Some of the most destructive phrases in the English language are: "I don't want to gossip, but . . ." "This is a secret, but . . ." "I'll just share this so you can be praying about it . . ." Don't share intimate secrets as prayer requests. If you have "tongue trouble," read the book of James. When your husband confides in you, and you feel you *must* discuss it with someone, talk to the Lord about it. Recite Psalm 141:3 to yourself (discussed in preceding chapter). This is the only way to tame the tongue.

Suggesting/Nagging

It is very difficult to open up and share your deepest thoughts and emotions with someone who is critical of you and is constantly trying to improve you. Fear of ridicule keeps many a husband from communicating with his wife. A communion of spirit can only be present when our husbands are confident of our loving acceptance of them. When we criticize them in front of others or nag them about the areas of their lives which displease us, they get the idea that it is impossible for them to impress or interest us anyway, so why try?

We must *never* criticize our husbands in front of others. Some women do this in an attempt to make themselves look better than their mates, but what they are really doing is causing others to think they made a mistake in choosing him in the first place. The result is usually that the sympathies of those in hearing distance will lie with the husband.

What we wives call "nagging" and what our husbands think it is often differs. We think we are hinting or suggesting, but when we hint or suggest more than once, it becomes plain old nagging. Even hinting "once" in a harping tone of voice is nagging. The Bible says that a nagging wife is worse than a constant dripping on a rainy day (see Proverbs 27:15 TLB). The antidote for nagging is also found in the Bible. "Fix your thoughts on what is true and good and right. Think about things that are pure and lovely, and dwell on the fine, good things in others. Think about all you can praise God for and be glad about" (Philippians 4:8 TLB).

Forgive and Forget

"A dry crust eaten in peace is better than steak every day along with argument and strife" (Proverbs 17:1 TLB). An unforgiving spirit fosters a noncommunicative atmosphere in the home. Recently, a couple whom we had not seen for five years visited with us and some mutual friends. Later, at another chance meeting of the couple who had been away, the husband said, "We really need to pray for the Jones's. When we were visiting with all of you, there was an undercurrent of bitterness between them that was not present when we moved away." Although both my husband and I had been aware of a problem between the Jones's, we had not mentioned it to anyone. Our friends' observation proves that bitterness is very difficult to hide. It leaves its mark on the face and the personality. If it is evident to those outside the home, how can we keep it from anyone who is close to us—and especially from each other? If you are bitter about something your husband has done in the past, he can sense it easily and it will block your communication. We need to ask God for His forgiveness for our husband, and to help us to forgive him. When we pray "forgive us our debts as we forgive our debtors" it's a good thing God doesn't take us literally. If He forgave us as we forgive others, we'd be in a heap of trouble!

Jesus told the story of a man who owed the king $10,000,00. The king ordered him sold into slavery for nonpayment of the debt, but he begged the king to be patient and promised to pay him in full. The king took pity on the man and cancelled the debt. After he left the king, the same man—whose debt had just been wiped off the books—went directly to a man who owed him $2,000.00 and demanded payment. The Living Bible says he even "grabbed him by the throat and demanded instant payment" (Matt. 18:28). Then the helpless man begged him to be patient, but his creditor had him arrested and put in jail. When the king heard about what had happened, he was furious and had the ungrateful man (whom he had forgiven) put into a torture chamber. And the conclusion of the story, Jesus said, "So shall my heavenly Father do to you if you refuse to truly forgive your brothers" (Matthew 18:23-35).

I had read this passage of Scripture many times and each time had found it hard to identify with the debtor. In today's jargon we would probably refer to him as being a "turkey." It seems impossible that anyone who had been treated so mercifully would be so merciless to another person. And then the truth dawned! We, as Christians, who have been forgiven *so much* by God are, on the whole, an unforgiving lot! A woman who has been the victim of an unfaithful husband says, "I just can't forgive him!" Or, a wife whose husband cuts down her Christianity feels justified in harboring bitterness against him for that. It's downright scary—when we think of God possibly disciplining us severely to teach us this lesson of forgivensss. When I put myself in the position of the "turkey," I didn't like being identified with him; and I pray that I will remember his plight any time I find myself with an unforgiving spirit toward another human being.

The Fiji Islanders are very proud of their ability never to forget a wrong done them. When another person commits an offense against one of these natives, he hangs a reminder of it from the ceiling of his hut. The first thing he sees when he awakens in the morning, and the last thing when he goes to bed at night, is the object calling to mind the unkind deed done to him by the other person. Small wonder those natives who have not become Christians are cannibals!

Search your heart and ask God to reveal to you any bitterness or unforgiveness that you are harboring deep inside. Then ask Him to help you to overcome it. This will clear the air and open the way to commune with your husband.

In the following chapters, we will attempt to find a solution to those problem areas where marriage partners disagree most. During several of the Fulfilled Woman Seminars, conducted by Toni Spry and me the women in attendance were asked to fill out a survey sheet, anonymously. One of the questions was: "In what areas do you and your husband disagree most?: Finances, child discipline, use of free time, your housekeeping, his work, friends, Christianity, other." Since all these areas were checked by many of the women, we will discuss each one separately as a potential trouble spot.

6

The Barrier of the Beloved Offspring

On the top of the list of disagreements causing barriers in communication between married couples was child discipline. More couples were having problems with this than over finances, which was anticipated to be the most troublesome subject.

Sam Strict and Linda Lenient

God's perfect plan is for a husband and wife to complement each other—for the strong points of one to balance the weak points of the other and vice versa. This makes two people with certain weaknesses into one strong, solid, whole unit. The problem is that, in the average home, there is usually one tough, strict disciplinarian and one easygoing, "let-it-all-hang out" opposite personality. One parent says "spank the daylights out of them" and the other counters "discipline them with love." Who is right? Both are correct! Children must be loved, but they must also be spanked when they misbehave. The Bible says so. However, the misguided parents pull against each other and don't reinforce the authority of the one doing the disciplining. As their disagreement becomes evident to the child, he begins to pit one against the other in order to escape punishment for his wrong behavior. If he can get his parents quarreling with each other, it will take their minds off *him!*

Sam Strict is thought by his wife, Linda Lenient, to be too cruel and harsh. When she points this out to him, he reacts by being more severe. Linda counteracts this by siding with the child, giving extra treats to make up for the discipline. In a women's Bible study I teach, attended by a large number of ladies, I asked for a show of hands of those who felt their husbands were either too lenient or too strict in the disciplining of their children. Every hand went up!

The Mitzvah and Torah Concept

I listened to some tapes recently, by Pastor Paul Steele of Valley Church in Cupertino, California, dealing with the Mitzvah and Torah concept of child discipline.[2] Those tapes settled, for me, a lot of questions about *who* was to discipline. We know that there are women who do all of the disciplining while their husbands play the "good guy" part; and there are others

2. Based on Proverbs 6:20-23. The word "command" is Mitzvah, "law" is Torah. The commandment was the lamp which is the basis of operation; the law is light, comparable to the flame of the candle which carries out the function of the lamp.

who refuse to reprimand their children at all but scare them to death by their "wait till your father gets home" threats. Neither of these is the right way.

The Mitzvah and Torah comes from the Hebrew law books. The Torah was the over-all principles and guidelines of the law such as the Ten Commandments. The Mitzvah was the execution of the law. For instance, the Torah would be "Thou Shalt Not Steal." The Mitzvah would be the details explaining what stealing is and the determination of the punishment.

The father in the home is to determine the Torah. He sets the goals and guidelines and determines the chores the kids should do, how late they should stay out—that is, the overall behavior patterns. The Mitzvah is the mother's job, for the most part, because she is home with the children by far the greater part of the time. She tells the son to mow the lawn, the daughter to do the dishes, sees that they come home from school on time, etc. Mother and Father discuss the rules beforehand and they back each other up in the execution of them. This does not mean that Father proclaims, "I want my kids to have good manners," and from then on leaves it up to their mother. They mutually decide that it is time to teach the children table manners and explain what is acceptable and what is not. When Mom is alone with the children, she continues this instruction; but, when Dad is home, he also teaches and they reinforce each other's authority. When discipline is necessary, the parent who is present should spank. If both parents are at home, it should be up to the father for he is the head authority in the home.

A good guideline for discipline and spanking is that when the child commits an offense after he has been given instruction and warning, the parent asks, "What did you do?" This forces the child to verbally admit his error and rids him of carrying around the guilt (i.e., "I hit my sister," or "I didn't clean my room when I was asked to do it"). The parent tells him it was a wrong thing to do, and that he must be punished. The spanking is done with a switch or rod, not in anger, but firmly on the buttocks until the child cries repentantly. (If he screams in a fit of anger, the spanking should continue until he cries softly.) Then the child is loved and cuddled by the parent and told he is forgiven. This is the biblical way, and the proper way to discipline. You may also find that my book *Family Love Story* is a helpful guide in dealing with adolescents and teenagers.

19 Principles in Training Children

Pastor Steele, who gave the mitzvah-torah concept, also shared with his ladies' Bible study group nineteen basic principles in training children. These are scriptural principles designed to keep the child in the will of God. If you have a committed Christian husband and young children, this will be easier for you to do. If your husband is not a Christian and/or your children are already older and giving you problems, it will be more difficult, but there has still been a good percentage of success reported with those who have diligently applied these principles in rearing their children. They are like any other biblical concept: If applied correctly, they will absolutely work out for God's best. However, we must realize there is always a measure of human error, and there will be ups and down in our application and follow-through. There is no better guide for raising our children in the nurture and admonition of the Lord than the Bible. The Scriptures backing the concepts are in parentheses and it will be necessary for you to look them up on your own. I'll simply give a paraphrased or condensed version of the reference to help you to understand the principle.

1. Dedicate your child to God. (I Samuel 1:27-28)

Hannah told the Lord that Samuel was His for as long as he lived. As you take this first vital step for your child's benefit, expect Satan to plague you with doubts. He may tell you that if you do it, the Lord will take the child home to heaven or he might hint that the mission field is the destination of your offspring and you will never see him again after he is grown. Expect this attack and determine to dedicate your child in spite of any doubts or questions you might have. Remember that God loves that child far more than you do, and He knows what's best for him.

2. Raise the child in the nurture and admonition of the Lord. (Ephesians 6:4)

The nurture means that the father is to apply the rod for discipline. Admonition comes from the mother and it means to encourage and to warn. Since Mom is the one who spends the most time with the child, it is often she who leads him to the Lord.

3. Teach an alertness to God's Spirit.

a. Teach him how to be filled with the Holy Spirit. (Ephesians 5:18) This simply involves confessing all known sin and asking God to fill him with His Spirit. This is the Source of power for the Christian faith. We will be powerless, weak Christians until we learn of the ministry of the Holy Spirit in our lives.

b. Teach him about God's peace. (Colossians 3:15) It is a remarkable gauge when something is wrong in our lives. If everything is right between the child and his Lord, he will have the promised peace that passes understanding. (Philippians 4:7)

c. Teach him not to grieve or quench the Holy Spirit. Grieving the Spirit comes from moral weakness and concerns sins of commission. When he is committing a moral wrong it will grieve the Spirit, as in Ephesians 4:30. "Quenching" the Spirit does not refer to committing certain wrongs, but to the sins of omission. When the Holy Spirit is nudging and directing your child a certain way, for him to ignore these proddings would be quenching the Spirit. (I Thessalonians 5:19)

4. Teach a sensitivity to your spirit. (Ephesians 6:1-3)

Be sure to show your grief and hurt when your children disappoint you. Don't use it as a manipulation to get them to follow your way, but when they commit an offense, let them know that it hurts you deeply. They should feel badly when they disappoint you. Many a child has been deterred from getting into trouble at the thought of hurting his parents. They should want to please those they love.

5. Develop in your child a hunger for God's Word. (Deuteronomy 6:6-9; Proverbs 22:6)

Teach him to memorize Scripture. Most good Sunday Schools have a memorization program with rewards or prizes. Pastor Steele says, "Sweeten it up if you must to give him a hunger." There is nothing wrong with a reward for a job well done and even if the child is paid for his Scripture memorization, it will stay in his mind and come back to him when he is tempted to do wrong. Memorize with him, if that will motivate him, and hang plaques with Scripture verses on them in his bedroom and throughout your home. What he sees all the time will make an impression on his mind.

6. Develop a healthy fear of God in him. (Proverbs 1:7)

By "fear," we mean an awareness of both the power and presence of God. Love must be taught, but within the whole character of God—the omnipotence, omnipresence, omniscience and sovereignty of His power. A fear of God is an awesome respect for His holiness and power. Those of us who love the ocean also fear it as we realize its power. The liberal teaching of simply a God of love removes the incentive to live a holy life because it says "You can do anything you want—God loves everyone! Everyone will get to heaven!" God is just and He will punish disobedience and we must teach this while teaching of His love, affection, comfort and more positive (from our standpoint) attributes.

7. Give your child a sense of destiny. (Ephesians 1:15-21)

Change his life-style by making him aware that he is a child of the King and has a heritage that is higher than the non-Christian. He has a power within him from the Holy Spirit that enables him to achieve what would be impossible without it.

8. Teach your child the value of the permanent vs. the passing. (1 John 2:15-17; Matthew 6:19-21, 33)

His goals will be different (and his ways of attaining them) when he realizes the importance of living for heaven as well as for God's glory here on earth. What may seem absolutely vital to his existence may take on lesser importance when weighed against eternal values. Being popular with a certain crowd in school may be a top priority for the non-Christian, but for the Christian, God's approval means more. Sacrificing his Christian principles for the temporary esteem of the world will cause him to be overcome with guilt and unable to function properly in any area of his life.

9. Train him to discern the character of others. (The entire book of Proverbs will teach him this.)

There is much said in Proverbs about the loose woman vs. the virtuous woman, the unrighteous man vs. the righteous, the fool vs. the wise man. As he learns what this book says by reading and re-reading it, he will be able to see through the scoffer and the fool who is wise in his own eyes and will not be misled by temporal values.

10. Teach him to be loyal.

Jeremiah 35 tells the story of the families of Rechab and how God blessed them because they obeyed their father completely. He is comparing them with the Israelites who refused to obey God and says to them, "Won't you learn a lesson from the families of Rechab?" Loyalty to the principles of his family, to God and to the Scriptures will enable your child to live a long life with the blessings of the Lord on what he does. It is important that he not be influenced by others to forsake his Christian upbringing.

11. Teach your child to stand alone.

Familiarize him with the stories of Joseph (Genesis 37-50) and Daniel (Daniel 6). God honors those who are courageous enough to stand for His principles, though all others forsake them. There may be classes in which your child will be assigned to read literature bordering on the pronographic and teachers who will ridicule him. Prepare him for this and stand behind him.

12. Saturate your child's mind with Scripture.

Read Psalm 119 and use the Scripture when you discipline and when you are talking with him quietly and praying with him. Make certain he knows how to defeat Satan by casting him away in Jesus' name when he is being attacked by fear, temptation or frustration.

13. Show your child the consequences of evil. (Proverbs 7:20-27; Psalm 73).

He may seem to be escaping punishment for wrongdoing for a time, but it will not go on forever. Read the book of Esther and point out what happened to Haman, who was hung on the gallows he had erected for an innocent man. There are many examples of movie stars who have lived immoral lives and ended up committing suicide; rock celebrities who died from overdoses of drugs, etc. Make sure your child is familiar with this concept.

14. Teach your child to share his faith. (Philip-

pians 2:15; Matthew 5:16, 1 Peter 3:15)

Sharing our faith is commanded by Jesus, and whether we are the brave sort who can walk up to strangers and share the gospel or we wait for opportunities to show that we live differently from non-Christians, our lives are a witness. Your child needs to know that he should live as a "light before men" and you can help him to do this by being a good example. Your life speaks more loudly to your child than anything you can say to him.

15. Teach your child to edify others. (Romans 14:19; 15:2)

Part of his purpose in life as a Christian, is to build up other believers. He will accomplish this not by criticism and pointing the finger at them, but by admonishing in love and encouraging. We are always to help the weaker brother and beating him over the head with our Bibles only makes him discouraged or rebellious.

16. Teach him the relationship between answered prayer and obedience. (1 John 3:22)

Disobedience is a definite hindrance to answered prayer. John understood this principle years before, and wrote about it in John 15:10. When we please God, He blesses us. That doesn't mean everything is perfect in our lives when we are obedient, but it does mean our lives will be joyful in spite of trials. God says if we obey, our cup will overflow. His joy doesn't depend upon our circumstances but upon our relationship to Him. We may not always get what we want, but we will get what is best for us. Disobedience brings trouble and woe; be sure to impress this upon your child's mind.

17. Support your child in fervent prayer. (James 5:16)

Pray for him faithfully every day. When thoughts of your child pop into your mind, pray for him. His protection, decisions, actions and reactions are dependent to a large degree upon your supportive prayer. There are countless true stories of offspring saved from dire circumstances or tragic ends because of a mother's prayers.

18. If he fails, restore him. (Galatians 6:1)

You don't have the right to judge your own child. Train him, pray for him, discipline him and love him. Remember all of your own failures and God's forgiveness to you. There is an old Indian proverb about not judging a brother until you have walked a mile in his moccasins. It holds true with a child, too. Each of us was created uniquely and individually by God and our responses are different, our temperaments and personalities cause us to react in various ways. We cannot say, self-righteously, "*I would never be guilty of that!*" We err even as mature Christians and we cannot know the pressures and influences our children have to contend with every day when they are not with us.

19. Teach him a love affair with wisdom. (Proverbs 8).

Wisdom is knowing and doing right. Teach him to covet wisdom and to ask for it, according to James 1:5. If he has wisdom, he will avoid many mistakes.

If there is anything that I would, personally, add to these 19 principles it would be to pray with your children daily. It's never too early or too late to start and it will not only teach them the miracle of answered prayer and the source of power in their lives, but it will build a beautiful relationship between you and them. Don't pray long-winded, high-sounding prayers, but just simple sentences in everyday language as you would speak to any dear parent.

If you are having problems with your children and you feel it is because your husband is too strict or too lenient, realize that God knew beforehand what kind of father your children would need and that He is in control of them. If your husband refuses to discipline at all, don't nag him—pray for him. Discuss the mitzvah-torah concept with him, and if he is willing to read the book of Proverbs, there are many Scriptures in it regarding child discipline (Proverbs 13:24, 19:18, 23:13-14, 29:17). If you sincerely feel that he is too strict, examine your own attitudes. Be perfectly honest and objective and, unless he is cruel to the point of physical abuse, your children probably need a strict father; and without one, might be in trouble with authorities in later years. Many of us mothers tend to be a little softhearted when it comes to punishment, but we shouldn't be. We need to thank the Lord that He provided our children with fathers who care enough about them to want them to grow up to be fine, law-abiding citizens. We're all familiar with the mother who smilingly says "My Johnny is just *all* boy!" as he swings from our chandelier, runs his little metal cars on our best end tables and drips his popsicle on our carpeting. Johnny can do no wrong as far as she is concerned—she is oblivious to his faults but she isn't doing him any favors. His teachers and employers will not see him through her eyes and Johnny will have a very difficult time adjusting to life!

United or Untied

Children were meant to bring joy into a marriage and unity to their parents. Realize that they are a gift from God and that He has loaned them to us for however many years they are destined to be in our care. We usually have about 18-21 years with them until they leave the nest and we are back where we started—just the two of us. If we have quarreled over children for the better part of our married life, we will have to start over and build a relationship with our husband that will carry us through our middle years with that same enthusiasm and joy which we approached our newlywed time.

7

Bickering About the Budget

"Do you want to be truly rich? You already are if you are happy and good. After all, we didn't bring any money with us when we came into the world, and we can't carry away a single penny when we die. So we should be well satisfied without money if we have enough food and clothing" (1 Timothy 6:6-8 TLB). The Bible paraphraser here uses the word "happy," but in the King James version it is "content." Contentment means: "a frame of mind which is completely independent of all outward and external things and which carries within itself the secret of happiness." Contentment never comes from the possession of external things but from an inward attitude toward life.

Most couples argue over money. Usually it is because they have allowed it to become their main objective in life. They both want the right to do certain things with their income and they cannot agree. It is essentially a power struggle. There is more involved here than the money itself—it goes back to the little child with his toy.

When his friend wants to play with the toy, he clutches it to himself and screams, "No, *Mine*." When the husband wants to spend a portion of the income on a car, boat, sporting equipment or investments and the wife wants to buy a larger home, new furniture, more clothes, more luxuries for the children, the problem isn't where the money goes. It is that neither wants to give up what they consider their "rights" to the money.

Mine Or Ours?

We have observed that in the case of the working wife, her possessiveness of her income is usually even greater than that of her husband. She wants to keep her salary for luxuries or put it into a separate account to use as she sees fit. I know this from experience. I had not worked since my husband graduated from college and when I received my first royalty check as an author, I had the distinct feeling that it was *mine* and even thought of putting it into a separate account. As the Lord tapped me on the shoulder, I realized that it was, like all of our money, just *that—our* money! Every penny my husband has earned his whole life has gone into our joint account and here I was, selfishly thinking that it was *my* money. It went into our bank account to be blended together with my husband's earnings, as has everything I've earned since. If you resent having to "pay bills" with your earnings, understand that your husband may have these same feelings at times. When God controls your purse strings, it is immaterial how the money is spent. When His perfect will with our finances is being accomplished, both parties are able to be content with the management of it.

What about tithing—the practice of giving at least 10 percent of your income to the Lord for His work? Is it simply an Old Testament rule that is no longer practical in this present age? According to the book of Acts, the New Testament church was a sharing, giving church. God doesn't *need* our money—the riches of the whole universe are His—but *we* need to give it to Him. Remember the rich man in the Bible (Luke 12:16-21) stored up his wealth and built bigger barns to hold it all? God was very unhappy with him and took his life. The Bible tells us that we should give the first part of all our income to the Lord and He will, in turn, protect our possessions from Satan. (Malachi 3:10-11) That's a comforting thought when we consider how quickly we could be stripped of all of our material possessions. A serious illness or disability, fire or natural disaster, lawsuit, economic collapse, theft—any of these could wipe out even the most affluent person. Ask several Christians who tithe and they will encourage you to try it and reap the many blessings God bestows upon those who practice this biblical principle.

On the other hand, what of the husband who is a poor manager and fritters away the income foolishly? What is the answer for the Christian wife married to an unbeliever who refuses to tithe? Thankfully, she does not have to assume responsibility for the stewardship of her husband. God knows her heart and her only response is the right attitude toward God and her husband. She must never nag him about tithing—that will only cause him to rebel and keep a tighter rein on his wallet. He needs to feel the freedom from any pressure she may put on him, unintentionally. God doesn't want her husband's money until he wants to give it, so she must pray and wait.

Grateful or Greedy

Husbands react in different ways toward the use of their money. We need to recognize why they respond as they do and take the right steps to help them to overcome their hang-ups. Our own attitudes are the most important to straighten out first.

Below are listed some questions which we can ask ourselves to determine whether much of the problem lies with ourselves.

1. When your husband informs you of a purchase he has made for himself without your knowledge, do you become angry?
2. Are you dissatisfied with your financial status and material possessions?
3. Are you envious of friends who are more blessed materially than you are?
4. Do you spend money and keep it a secret from your husband?

5. Do you spend more than you should on the children?
6. Are you wasteful?
7. Do you buy things you need or things you "want" more often?
8. Do you have a desire to work outside the home in order to have more luxuries?
9. Do you believe your husband to be too stingy with your clothing allowance?
10. How many of your prayers center around financial matters?

If you answered "yes" to any of these questions, that is an area you need to pray about. God can take the desire for material wealth from you and replace it with a desire for spiritual wisdom and growth. These will bring you greater joy and contentment in the long run than any amount of material possessions. As your own attitude changes toward these things, you will probably find that your husband's attitude will change, too. This is an important step to solving the budget bickering.

Husband's Hang-ups

Before we delve into our husband's hang-ups, it would be well to do a little more self-examination. There is a difference between a husband who is selfish and one who is merely concerned, who is trying to curb unnecessary spending. Many wives have no concept of money and if your husband pays the bills and handles the finances, he may be aware that you have much less to spend than you think you do. Trust

God with your needs, in this case, and pray for a change of attitude. Ask the Lord to curb your desire for the things you can't afford.

We have met women who think their husbands spend too much, but on deeper acquaintance with the wives, have found that they are overly worried about money and not trusting that their husbands know the needs and are able to provide for them. One woman, who was so frugal that when she opened her wallet moths flew out, nagged her husband for any spending he did on the extras in life even though he was very wealthy. They lived the same as a family on an extremely tight budget, even to spending as little as possible on Christmas and birthdays, while storing great hordes of money in the bank "for a rainy day." It is good to have some savings but God expects us to enjoy whatever material blessing He chooses to give us.

There are husbands, however, who have serious problems with money. Let's investigate them here and try to give some helpful hints on how to react to these different types.

Tom Tightwad. Tom may allow you to have a joint checking account, but he usually carries the checkbook with him. He is the type who puts his wife on an allowance and never "allows" for inflation, unexpected expenses, a new piece of furniture or appliance unless the old has been declared by a jury of service men to be totally beyond repair. When you ask him for money, even for a necessity, it's like demanding a pint of blood, and he seldom gives it to you without an argument and many postponements. He absolutely hates paying for personal service, such as a repairman, waitress tips, doctor or dentist bills, etc. and feels that they are taking advantage of him. In fact, his main concern in life is that everyone is out to get his money and each time he is forced to give some of it to someone, it reduces his value as a person. His stinginess is a result of his feeling inadequate; and, by his standards, the more money he has, the more his self-worth increases.

It is easy to respond to his miserly and critical attitudes by pointing out to him that he is wrong. However, this only makes him worse and more determined to prove himself right. Look beyond his actions to why he is acting this way. A local disc jockey remarked on his program the other day, "Ladies, if you want to feel like a queen, treat your husband like a king!" There is more truth in that than he realized. Your husband is seeking approval and acceptance and possibly making up for a materially deprived childhood. He may have felt inferior to others because of a lack of money while growing up and thinks riches are the answer to being admired by his peers. He needs your thoughtful reflection, your strength in resisting his intimidation and your willingness to accept him just as he is, with his weaknesses as well as his strengths. When you ask him for money or for something new and he says no, respond with the right attitude—a big smile and something like "You know best, honey." Don't pout! Remember that God is in control. He will either change your husband's mind (if you accept his decision willingly and refuse to nag) or you didn't need whatever it was, anyway.

Sam Spender. It's probably a toss-up as to which is the more difficult to live with—Sam Spender or Tom Tightwad. Sam takes the opposite approach from Tom's possessiveness of money. He doesn't care about it at all! It is made to have fun with, in Sam's opinion, and he has no conception of his responsibility to God concerning its use. He is completely irresponsible and makes snap decisions to buy things he cannot afford. We once had a neighbor who had just had his car repossessed and was in danger of losing his home for overdue mortgage payments when he spent $1500 on a piano. (Incidentally, no one in the family could play the piano!) When he was discussing this with my husband and me, I asked, "Whatever possessed you to buy a piano when you are having such financial problems?" He replied, matter of factly, "That's just the way I am, Lou!" His family eventually lost their home (including the piano) and the last we heard of them, they had moved to another town where he began his buying sprees all over again with a new set of bank loans!

In most cases, "Sam's" wife works, takes over the finances and tries to keep up with bailing him out of his jams. As a Christian, you can claim God's protection against financial disaster, but it is important to let your husband take the lead without playing "mother" to him. Perhaps his spending habits came from over-indulgent parents or from a lack of discipline in his youth. Give him the right to fail—maybe he needs to do just that for the Lord to wake him up to his responsibility to his family. When you manage his affairs for him, you are supporting his destructive behavior. That's what our neighbor's wife did. She would arrange with the creditors to sell something to pay them off, or refinance their car or home, and her husband felt no responsibility to change. Since neither of them were Christians, it was almost impossible for them to work things out. But, as a child of God, you can pray for your husband and, without nagging him, see God change him. Trust God to overrule when your husband has gone too far, and be loving, uncomplaining and submissive. Tell your mate that since he is the head of the house, you will refer all calls from creditors to him so he can take care of them. You will write the checks if he wishes, but the ultimate financial decisions must be up to him. When he hurts enough, he will change.

Guidelines to Money Conflicts[3]:

1. Face them while they're fresh. Don't put off your discussion till later. Suppressing your feelings is not healthy. You may want to choose

3. James Kilgore, *Getting More Family Out of Your Dollar* (Irvine, CA., Harvest House Publishers, 1976), p. 120.

the best time for discussion—after the children are in bed—definitely not when your husband is extra tired and hungry. Pray for a loving attitude as you communicate.

2. Discuss in the present tense. Stick to the issue at hand, not what happened last week or last year. Don't sidetrack and bring up complaints about other areas of your marriage.

3. Deal with the conflict courteously. Don't walk away, yell or withdraw. If your husband yells at you, lower your voice. This will cause him to lower his, too, and also will tone down the conversation and make it less emotional. Courtesy demands attention to what is being said. Don't ignore, slam doors, bang drawers or cry.

4. Listen as much as you talk. You need to understand your husband's point of view. Listening helps you to understand. Ask him to repeat a point if you don't feel you completely grasp his meaning or intent. Sometimes we simply watch his mouth and don't hear what he's saying because we're thinking of what we're going to say next. You may hear things differently when you really listen. Don't "see red" when he criticizes you without listening to all of what he says—he may say something nice and you'll miss it! Write thoughts down, if necessary, to keep them in order so that you may answer his points without getting mixed up.

5. Negotiate naturally. Be willing to compromise. Not: "My mind is made up . . . don't confuse me with the facts!" Ask yourself: "What steps can I take to make the problem less

painful? Does my husband have a good point? How can we be closer together in our differences? How do I want this settled?''

6. Bury the hatchet. Do your best to reconcile the differences. End on a loving note. We as wives are not responsible for what our husbands do with the money — only what we ourselves do.

Read *Getting More Family Out Of Your Dollar* with your husband. It is not a ''religious'' type book that would turn off a non-Christian husband. Dr. Kilgore is a Christian psychologist, however, so his book is written from a Christian standpoint, and is most helpful in understanding money problems and solving them.

With the ''barrier of the budget'' broken down, communication will be much easier within your marriage. When both of you are disturbed about financial matters, it is difficult to be open about your feelings in other areas. It's like having a sore toe. You still have two good feet but walking is difficult until that one little toe is healed. We need to heal this troublesome area of our marriages in order to have close communication in every facet.

8

"Free-for-all" Time

A letter was received by a daily columnist in our newspaper which read, in part: "Women take so many tranquilizers because they are nervous and have too much time on their hands. Blame it on modern, pushbutton living."

The response to that statement was overwhelming. The columnist received a deluge of mail from women readers with comments ranging from a list of duties of the housewife (bibs, diapers, noses to wipe, tears to stop, playtime, preventing quarrels, housework, balancing meals, dishes, shopping, sewing, cleaning, gardening, a husband to please, mending neighborhood friendly fences, church work, school duties, etc.) to several insisting that the letter had to have been written by a man! One woman wrote, "I have 12 children and a 12-room house. This push-button existence of which she writes is a riot!" Another letter included the story of the midwestern farmer whose wife was taken to an insane asylum. He wrote, "What did she have to go crazy about? She hasn't been out of her kitchen in 20 years."

A Time To Play

"Time On My Hands" was a popular song in the 40s (for all of you youngsters who weren't born yet), but undoubtedly would never make it big today. Time on our hands is something nobody seems to have anymore. And what little extra time we do have seems to cause disagreement in many marriages. "How to spend our free time" was checked as a source of irritation by a large percentage of the women who completed the marriage survey which was mentioned in chapter five.

In order to offer a possible solution, to free-time management, we need to examine the problem. One area of disagreement, the survey showed, was the type of vacation the family should take. Some complained that their husbands went hunting or fishing with the boys and they were forced to take separate holidays. Others said they argued over how to spend their weekends or even free time in the evenings. There were those who said every vacation meant visiting relatives. Some husbands spent all weekend on the golf course, tennis courts, fishing, hunting, bowling, etc., leaving their wives at home.

If your husband has two days off, you might try having a heart-to-heart talk with him when he's in a good mood. Suggest that he have one day for his favorite activities and one day for the family. A man needs some time to himself, just as we women do.

In fact, there is an alternative for us, too. If you are financially able, how about hiring a good baby-sitter and setting aside one day every week or two to spend exactly as you please? If this is out of the question, do you have a relative in town who will spell you in this way? (If you do have one, be sure to repay her in thoughtful ways such as homemade goodies, running some errands for her, or helping her with her housework one day.) If there are no relatives nearby, talk with a friend or neighbor and offer to trade off baby-sitting. One week, you take her children for the day and the next week she can take yours.

If you are a mother whose children are in school, you can feel free to spend your "day off" from the time they leave in the morning until they come home. Do whatever pleases you. However, make certain you organize your home so that it doesn't suffer in the interim. You can do this by spending less time on the telephone or neighboring, by making lists and getting your shopping done quickly, no daytime TV, etc. As long as the wash, housework and meals are kept up, your husband probably won't mind your taking a day off. Don't assume you are stuck at home and can never have any fun. There are creative alternatives to everything if we just take time to explore them.

Happy (?) Holidays

The question of what kind of vacations to take

can be the cause of the wrong kind of communication (quarreling) or no communication at all. If your vacation planning sessions end up in a deadlock each year, let's determine the reason. Often this annual hassle is due to a difference of what each partner thinks a vacation should be. Most husbands love to go camping, but many wives absolutely refuse to join them. "It's worse than being home," they say. "At least there we have dishwashers, electric ranges and our own bathroom!"

I can sympathize with the mother who goes camping with several small children and cooks on a Coleman stove, washes dishes by lantern and trudges off to a cold bathroom with her flashlight late at night. It is easier to manage when you are at home, but if you ask the Lord to help you to relax and enjoy camping, you will find it to be the highlight of each year.

When we asked our grown children recently what they considered to be the most fun of anything we did as a family, we expected to hear "our trips to Disneyland" or "when we stayed at that resort" etc. The unanimous answer, however, was "our camping trips!" I believe these family times were enjoyed most because we were so casual on these outings. Everyone wore old clothes, there was no pressure, and we had real "togetherness." A big pot of spaghetti, cooked on the Coleman stove, tasted better than a lobster dinner in a posh restaurant. We used paper plates so there wouldn't be too many dishes, and we had lots of free time to fish, wade in a stream, watch an ant colony stock its winter supplies, pick wildflowers, hike, attend the ranger's campfires at night to watch the skits and nature films, play games at the picnic table, and sing songs to my very bad ukelele playing around the campfire (before our youngest son became an expert guitarist). Those were precious, precious times together and I wouldn't trade them for anything.

If you are absolutely miserable camping and paranoid about bugs and dirt, stay in a cabin or recreation vehicle (trailer or motor home) in the woods so your husband and kids can be outside most of the time and you can be comfortable. The next time you plan for your vacation, think of the words to this song by Bill and Gloria Gaither. It may help you to realize what is most important, in the long run.

"Hold tight to the sound of the music of living
Happy songs from the laughter of children at play
Hold my hand as we run through the sweet fragrant meadows
Making mem'ries of what was today.
We have this moment to hold in our hands
And to touch as it slips through our fingers like sand;
Yesterday's gone and tomorrow may never come,
But we have this moment today.[4]

4. Gaither, William J. and Gloria. "We Have This Moment Today" (Gaither Music Co.) 1975.

"Mini-Moons"

Our daughter, Nancy, and her husband, Jim, recently attended a marriage seminar given at the college where he is studying for the ministry. One good idea presented at the seminar, which they shared with us, was taking "mini-moons" — short, overnight honeymoons — once or twice a year. If it's financially possible to take longer ones, this would be great! But if the budget is at a straining point, save your money for six months and make reservations at a motel in a nearby town or resort area. Have dinner at a restaurant, put on a frilly nightie, and have your mini-moon. If you know someone with a cabin in the mountains or at the beach, ask if you can borrow or rent it for a night. Take along some steaks, the makings of a salad and have dinner by candlelight. Recently one couple even took a mini-moon at our home while we were out of town for the weekend. We appreciated having them house-sit and they enjoyed the change of scenery, the swimming pool and the water bed. There are many inexpensive ways to take these mini-moons; so if you don't have relatives or a competent baby-sitter nearby, how about trading with a friend for these?

Just as important as mini-moons is scheduling a time each week for you to be together with your husband, alone. Hire a teenager in your neighborhood to baby-sit for a couple of hours, go bicycle riding, for a walk in the park, or just to a coffee shop and talk. If you can afford to go out to dinner, this is a great way to have a time of intimate sharing. Be sure you don't get into the habit of *always* going out with another couple. This is easy to do when you have close friends with whom you enjoy spending time. Married couples have a need to be alone and we should make it a point to see that we take this time often. If you are faithful to do this, you will find your relationship taking on a new dimension as you get to know each other again.

Taming the TV

There are many factors which contribute to the "stone wall of silence" in a marriage, but one culprit stands out like a sore thumb. It is the TV—or rather, the misuse of it! God forbid that we should become legalistic and recommend that all of you throw your television sets in the trash can. TV is often entertaining, great for watching sports events and educational programs, and a blessing for those who are disabled, lonely and alone. But television is like any other blessing: If allowed to get out of hand, it becomes a curse. It subtly takes over our lives until we are spending nearly all of our free time, plus a lot of time that should be spent on more important tasks, staring into what is affectionately called "the boob tube." Any hobby can become as demanding as the TV, but watching television is the most convenient, accessible and effortless way to spend time, and we can become "hooked" before we realize it.

In the *Fulfilled Woman Marriage Survey*, the women rated the communication in their marriages as "poor," "fair," "needs improving," "good," or "fantastic." In the "poor to fair" group, over half of the women watched TV more than an hour a day and one-fourth of them watched from two to three-and-one-half hours of daytime TV. In this same group, 75 percent of the couples spent from two to five hours per night in front of the television set. At the opposite end of the scale, in the "fantastic" communication group, *none* of the women watched daytime TV and 70 percent of the couples either watched no TV at all or less than an average of one hour per night! The first group, when asked to rate their marriages on a scale of 1 to 10 (10 being "the greatest"), put down an average score of 4.5. All of the second group (the minimum TV watchers) rated their marriages at either 9 or 10.

Mis-Use Makes Misery

What do these figures prove? I definitely do not believe that it is conclusive that all those who watch TV will end up with marital problems! I simply feel that this could be a contributing factor to a lack of communication in the home. It would be hard to believe that a wife who spent all of her spare time watching soap operas, game shows or reruns would be a very stimulating conversationalist when her husband comes home in the evening. Chances are that if the TV is on when her husband arrives, it will stay on till bedtime. Even if, as some women indicated, they watch mostly Christian TV, it is still one of the world's greatest time-wasters. Two hours can go by so fast it seems like but a few moments. I realize that reading, sewing, painting, crafts—any hobby—can be time-consuming, and can easily get out of proper priority. But nearly every other hobby comes to an end! The book is finished, the picture completed, the sweater knitted, the tennis game played. Television just goes on and on and on and on.

Much of what is shown on TV is unfit for Christians to watch. Violence, sex, sadism, off-color jokes, depressing stories—It's difficult to choose what is proper material to put into our heads and what is not. We don't know until we begin watching a program if it is going to be suggestive or violent, and it's much harder to turn the dial once we become interested in the plot.

The women's magazines and the pro-uncensored TV groups would have us believe that sex on the screen would help us to be better adjusted, more "turned-on" wives. Our women's survey shot holes in their theory as the TV-watchers group rated their sex lives "needs improving" or "do not enjoy it" with only one rating of "satisfactory" and one of "terrific." Of the occasional watchers, 80 percent rated their sex lives as "terrific" and the remainder "satisfactory." We don't have to fill our minds with suggestive material to have a terrific sex life. Filling it with Scripture works far better!

Television not only is a barrier to the communication of couples who have been married for a time, but even to newlyweds. As they sit viewing the programs each evening, there is no time for conversation unless they want to out-shout the commercials. Those of us who were married in the pre-TV era spent hours talking each night, just getting to know each other. Our daughter and son-in-law, who have been married a little over two years, have never had a TV and don't even miss one. Some evenings they talk until 2:00 a.m. and have never yet had a communication problem. Since he is studying for the ministry, he spends many evenings hitting the books, but they still find time to talk, play games, go for walks, or bike rides, have friends over, read (and share what they are reading). Now they say they have no intention of *ever* buying a television set. It is understandable why so many young couples have marital problems when they spend their free hours in noncommunication, in front of the TV set. For those who have a television, it is important to use it wisely and refrain from becoming addicted to it.

Creative Distraction

Unfortunately, there are many women who don't particularly enjoy TV whose husbands are addicted to it. What is the answer here? What must we do to compete with millions of dollars worth of programming and the LA Rams? As far as the Rams go, we'd suggest, "Let him watch his sports!" There is no way you are going to get his mind off those games, and the most logical answer would be to become interested and enjoy them with him. Fortunately, there is a limit to sports viewing. There *are* times when there simply aren't any sports programs available to watch. This, then, is when we take the offensive. We can make our husbands aware of us—even if we have to start during the commercials. Or, we can capture their attention during, or right after, dinner . . . or after TV—when it's time to go to bed. We can dress in feminine attire, with his favorite cologne. We can "cuddle up a little closer." We can ask questions about the game he has just watched (most men love to do "instant replays" of all the exciting moments of the games—sort of relive them). We can admire and compliment him; fix him extra snacks; or present him with a surprise gift he's been wanting (*not* a new TV set). We can suggest playing games, if he enjoys them (Scrabble, Sentence-Cubes, Yahtzee, Score Four, to name a few games that most men like). Ask the Lord to help you to be creative in thinking up ideas to get your husband's attention, and his mind off the TV. And when all else fails, pray for the TV to do likewise!! (At least a "week-in-the-shop" type failure.)

If you, yourself, are a dyed-in-the-wool TV

watcher, ask God to help you get your priorities straight and to give you the strength to push the "off" button—or, better yet, the strength to resist pushing the "on" button! Relax with a good book. There are thousands of excellent Christian books on the market, and if you don't like "heavy" reading, try some of the autobiographies by Joyce Landorf, Dale Evans, Anita Bryant, Norma Zimmer, Corrie Ten Boom, Joni Eareckson, Maria Ann "Hansi" Hirschmann. These books are easy to read and have a message to our hearts.

If you are not a reader, and don't enjoy it, spend your time doing something like: crewel embroidery pictures (there are small ones in the stores that are easy for beginners and they make great gifts); crocheting an afghan, knitting a sweater, quilting, sewing; gardening, growing houseplants in clever containers for gifts; refinishing furniture, or bringing your photograph albums up to date. Those of you who are artistic probably need no encouragement to paint, make pottery, macrame plant hangers, flannel pictures, memorabilia boxes, dried flower arrangements, or terrariums. Many of these projects don't even require a lot of talent, and you may find you have hidden abilities when you get started.

If you like to write letters, try your hand at a short story or even a book. If you're musical, play the piano or another instrument (but not in the same room where your husband is watching football!).

If daytime TV is your problem, leave the house and go for a walk, play a game of tennis, or ride your bike. Join a gym where you can exercise indoors in the winter. Get involved in your church or a worthwhile community project. Once the TV habit is broken, you will find that you won't want to return to it because life is too much fun without it.

Gear your free time to improving your communication with your husband, not stifling it. Adapt to his interests and you will find him adapting to yours—and your holidays, weekends and evenings together will enhance your marriage relationship.

9

Actions and Reactions

Now that we've learned some of the steps we can take as wives to improve our attitudes and heal the trouble spots in our marriage, is there any special way to react to different types of husbands? We all have friends whose husbands are easy communicators—especially if they have been blessed with some sanguine[5] in their temperament. I've never met a noncommunicative sanguine—their main problem is that they over-communicate! In other words, they never stop talking. If you're married to a man with a sanguine temperament, count your blessings. At least, life is never boring!

Noncommunicators, however, fall into several different groups and subgroups. I've listed some of these more common personalities with whom you may be able to identify.

Barry Blow-yer-top. Barry is the strong, silent type until something makes him angry. Then, *watch out!* He lashes out with more words than

5. Sanguine qualities: talkative, outgoing, enthusiastic.

you have heard from him all month—but they're not what you'd been hoping to hear. When he's through spouting off, he retreats again behind his wall of silence without giving you a chance to respond. Hopefully, you do not scream back at Barry—that only makes things worse. Proverbs 15:1 says "a soft answer turneth away wrath," and it's hard to stay mad at someone who doesn't return our anger. If an apology is in order, for whatever caused Barry's anger, then offer one. If it was something you did unintentionally, apologize for that, too, and ask God for a special portion of love for him. He probably hates his temper even worse than you do. You can help your spouse to correct this bad habit of anger *with your knees,* not your mouth. Prayer changes things!

Barry finds it hard to discuss problems without becoming angry. Nagging or arguing only make his problem worse. If his anger becomes so violent that he physically abuses you, then professional counseling is in order, either from your minister, doctor, or psychologist. However, make sure that your attitude isn't the reason for his anger. Look beyond what he's saying to why he's saying it. Is he physically well? Is he unhappy in his job? Does he have insecurities which you could alleviate by building him up and admiring him?

My husband had a very bad temper the first few years we were married. He was never physically abusive, but he became angry over everyday frustrations and it was impossible to reason with him. When I finally caught hold of the concept of being a submissive wife and admiring him verbally, his temper began to disappear. Now he is often asked how he stays so mellow, even when those around him in business are falling apart and losing their cool. He always answers that it is the Lord who made him that way—and He did (through showing me how to be the right kind of wife). Do you cause your husband to feel inferior or unloved? A contented man is not an angry man. Look for the cause of his discontent and you will have the solution to his anger.

Stanley Silent. Stanley listens (or seems to) when you talk, but seldom comments. He is quiet, not only at home, but with others, too. When you were going together, you admired his silent strength and he seemed to enjoy your bubbly, talkative personality. The twinkle in his eye and the way he looked at you gave you assurance that he was listening and enjoying it. After a few years, however, the twinkle disappeared and was replaced by a look of boredom. (One-sided conversations are always boring, aren't they?) After spending the day with three little ones, under six years of age, a longing for adult conversation pervades your whole being. A grunt is hardly conversation. You could get more action than that out of the dog—at least he wags his tail and appears glad for the attention.

Stanley is a sweet husband, a good provider, obviously fond of his children, conscientious about keeping up your home, and generous to a fault. He simply does not satisfy your need for communication. When he does talk with you, it is simply surface information. "It rained today," he comments (as if you didn't know that—you had to drive Junior to school). When you ask him questions, he replies with one-word answers, declining to comment further.

Stanley Silent is also Stanley Stay-at-home. Getting him out of the house on weekends is like dragging the dog to the vet—you end up having to carry him inside. But Stanley is too heavy for you to carry anyplace. Besides, you'd feel silly heaving him across the threshold into someone's house or through the doors of a restaurant. He feels his home is his castle, and he is content to spend his nonworking hours there—either puttering in the garage, watching TV or snoozing on the sofa. You've come to the point where you wish he'd yell at you—anything for some attention!

Stanley obviously has problems in self-acceptance. He feels insecure conversing. Perhaps he has been ridiculed at some time for his ideas, or is carrying around some traumatic experience from childhood that caused him to withdraw into himself. He not only has problems in the area of self-acceptance, he has a large dose of self-centeredness! He's not aware of the boredom and frustration you feel spending night after night shut out of his life by his self-protective silence.

Stanley may respond to admiration, warmth and a little humor. He may open up to questions about his job or some other subject that particularly interests him. If you have "clammed up" in response to his "clamming up" over the years, that could be part of the problem. Seek God's help in viewing Stanley through His eyes and in discerning the reasons for his lack of communication. If it is a lack of self-confidence, you—as his wife—can help him a great deal in this area. It will mean risking failure and rejection on your part. And should he fail to respond, at first, don't take it personally. Instead, ask God to grant you additional discernment and creative ideas to draw your husband out. Concentrate on Stanley and not yourself. This will help him to see you in a new light and revive that old twinkle in his eye.

Ned Never Home. A problem in many households today is the man who has a job demanding a large amount of travel. In many sales jobs, not only must the husband travel but he also finds himself entertaining customers in his "off hours." All this *may* be necessary, but in many instances, it's a good excuse to get away from home. If this is your situation, ask yourself, "Does he *really* need to be gone as much as he is, or have I made the type of home from which he would just as soon be absent?" Vicki's husband is a salesman and he will do absolutely *anything* to finagle a way to be home at night. He will get up at 4:30 a.m. to drive to a town three hours away, schedule appointments as close together as possible, and drive home the same night—arriving as late as 9:00 p.m. in order to keep from being gone from his wife and family. If he *must* take a customer for dinner, he invites Vicki to join them. He does most of his business entertaining over the lunch table rather than at dinner. Yet, he knows dozens of other salesmen who will purposely take three or four days to work with customers in the same city he covers in a day. They schedule their appointments to include dinner and nights out "on the town." They must not have the kind of home to return to that I do!" he says, when questioned about it. He looks forward to returning to the warmth of his neat home, well-prepared meals, the loving welcome from his wife and children and the appreciation they show for his extra efforts on their behalf. If he is later than expected, he knows there will be no nagging, only gratitude that he made it home. He looks forward to the amusing stories of the day's events and the sincere interest in his travels and customers. His wife has learned how to bring her husband home, not with whining and cajoling and complaining, but with love and admiration and appreciation. Proverbs 12:4 says, "A virtuous woman is a crown to her husband" and Vicki has learned how to be that crown.

Tim Turned-off. Tim wasn't the quiet type

when you were first married, but he is changing. He seems to have become disinterested in you and he is not nearly so affectionate as before. He may even leave you sitting alone at get-to-gethers while he turns on the charm for others. He doesn't ask you to go many places with him anymore, and he often works late. Why the change?

A very touchy subject among us women is our appearance. When the Bible speaks of being "a new creature" (2 Corinthians 5:17), how about taking it literally? Could the reason Tim Turned-off no longer hurries home be that, compared with the girls in his office, we don't score too well? Wherever a man works—even in construction—be sure there are girls (in these days of women's lib). And wherever there is more than one woman, you can be certain each is conscious of her appearance. Recently, a lady meter-reader came to our home, and even with her PG&E uniform, she looked attractive. Her hair was clean and shining, her uniform pressed, her face made up, and she filled out her uniform in all the right places.

The Pound Problem

There are very few women over 35 who are at an ideal weight. We don't mean that we should all be sporting the starved look of the fashion models—the emaciated, thin woman has a weight problem, too (but to the other extreme).

Next time you are grocery shopping, notice the number of women who are considerably overweight. Gaining pounds is the cross many of us must bear and it's a constant struggle with diet, diet, diet! We could count the friends on one hand who don't have to watch their weight carefully. If your communication with your husband is poor, try losing your extra pounds and see if it doesn't pick up. Even 10 pounds of extra weight can add years to your appearance.

I would not recommend fad diets, nor any kind of diet, without your doctor's okay. The one way that seems to work best in keeping weight stable is a plain old 1,000 calorie diet. I feel carbohydrate diets are dangerous to the health because of the large amount of high-cholesterol foods consumed; and the faddish diets which take off weight very quickly work for a short time, but rarely have a lasting effect. Diet pills are hard on the heart, and the "diet doctors" who advertise are often not qualified M.D.'s and very unethical in their practice and use of pills, shots and other medication. A balanced diet of lean meat, vegetables, fruit and a small amount of fat to act as a catalyst is good for your health and will establish a new pattern of eating. Weight Watchers works on this same principle and is excellent if you have a lot of pounds to lose. Most people diet a little and cheat a lot. My doctor says we should diet a lot and cheat a little!

Keeping busy is a big help in breaking the

habit of eating between meals. Try writing down everything you eat (and at what time) for a three-day period, and be prepared to be embarrassed when you see how much! Notice what time you are likely to snack and choose an alternative for that hour. I do pretty well all day and evening except for a period around 4:00 p.m. when I am tired, beginning to get hungry, and it's too early to start dinner. In the summer, I swim laps at this hour, and by the time I get dried off, shower, and dress, it's time to prepare dinner. If it isn't swimming weather, a walk is a good idea. Once around the block will take your mind off the food. If the weather is bad, I practice the piano. It makes me concentrate and I don't think about food. Find something to keep yourself busy at these times when you are tempted to eat. (But don't go to the grocery store—you'll buy everything in sight.)

Instead of a sandwich for lunch, try having a big salad in the summer time (25-50 calories instead of 350 for a sandwich); in the winter, a bowl of soup is about 100 calories at the most and is more nourishing and filling. Fresh fruit is good for you and satisfies that craving for sweets. Unless your husband insists, don't keep a constant supply of pie and cakes in the house. If he likes ice cream, try serving that each night for dessert, saving the fancy stuff for company when they will finish it off and you won't be tempted by leftovers. Put a sign on the cookie jar reminding yourself they're for the kids and ask the Lord to nudge you when you absentmindedly begin to reach for a snack.

I'm convinced there would be a lot of rejuvenated marriages if there were some rejuvenated figures on the wives. If your husband is overweight, he will likely be happy to join you on your diet. Most men are as self-conscious about looking good as women. Maintaining your proper weight will do wonders for your self-image, too. You will be more confident at meeting new people, more assured in your relationship with your husband, and a better witness for Christ. When you are tempted to go on a food binge remember: Eat it today, wear it tomorrow!

Good Looking and Looking Good

Appearance is more than weight, however. It is cleanliness, good grooming and caring how we look. What does your husband see when he leaves in the morning? When he comes home at night? Do you send him off with curlers in your hair, no makeup, a shabby robe, halitosis and sleep in your eyes? When he arrives home from work, are you in old jeans and a sweatshirt, with the same curlers in your hair and no makeup?

I get up early enough to brush my teeth, comb my hair, put on a little lipstick and blusher, a pretty robe, and cook breakfast for my husband. I give him lots of kisses before he leaves and sometimes, for laughs, I sit on his foot, hugging his knee and beg him not to go! It sends him off in a good humor and starts my own day on a jolly note. Whenever I go shopping—even to the grocery store three blocks away, I put on a well-tailored pair of pants, blouse, sweater, makeup, jewelry and cologne because I am representing my Lord and my husband. I don't want people to look at me in disgust, saying "That's a Christian? What a mess!" It takes a little more effort and an extra load of wash each week, but it's worth it for the compliments I get from my husband. Even if your husband is the unobserving type, and doesn't think to mention how nice you look, he will appreciate your looking nice, and you will feel a self-confidence you don't have when you're looking tacky.

We, as wives, need to realize that as we get older the ratio of women to men gets much higher. By the time we are in our 40s there aren't nearly enough men to go around. With women penetrating every facet of business and industry today, the opportunities for our husbands to be tempted increases. We have to be on our toes and practice "heads-up" housewifery—excelling at what God has given us the ability to do best: please that man we married!

The Absentee Husband

I received a letter recently from a trucker's wife who wanted answers to the problem of being both mother and father while her husband is away. She said it is very difficult to relinquish her authority when her husband comes home. This would also apply to servicemen's wives and others whose husbands must travel for long periods of time. (Anything over three days is a long period of time to me!) The only solution I can offer is prayer—for your attitude, and for help in being submissive when he is home. Discuss your problem with your husband and ask his help in reminding you that he is the authority when he is present.

We have one delightful friend whose husband is a construction superintendent in a national firm. He is gone for weeks and even months at a time, depending upon where the firm is building. (They construct shopping centers throughout the country.) He flies home for weekends periodically and his wife flies to be with him once a month; but, when he is home, their schedule undergoes a drastic change. She completely turns the reins over to him, caters to his wishes and makes his stay as pleasant, romantic and exciting as possible. The children fall into gear with their mother's mood and treasure the time spent with their father. It is a difficult way to live, to be sure, but God has given this gal the grace to cope with it. She is very involved with her church, as are her children, and they take in conferences and speakers and programs at other churches in the area to fill the long hours while her husband is away.

We must ask God for wisdom in gearing our lives to our husband's occupation and let Him guide us in our individual circumstances. No two families or situations are the same; therefore, the rules cannot be hard and fast to apply to every family. Only the principles and concepts of God's Word are unchanging. Remember that God knows your particular dilemma, your family unit and personalities, and He can give you a fulfilled life no matter what seemingly insurmountable obstacles are present.

10

Quenching the Quarrel

Charlie Shedd says, "Marriage is not finding the right person; it's *being* the right person." And being the right person means being open and honest about your feelings. Most every divorce began in a point of time when one or both partners decided not to tell the whole truth. We need to be able to share our problems openly, lovingly. We shouldn't be afraid to ask our mates to tell us what traits in us they feel need improving. *But*, we must listen and pray as they are telling us. If we argue, defend or refute, we aren't listening—we're reacting—and this can lead to quarreling. Realize that this is not just your husband speaking, but is God speaking *through* your husband. And God can never tell us anything unless we are quiet and listening. Your husband is trying to help you to mature, he's not trying to start a quarrel.

The dictionary defines a quarrel as "verbal strife in which angry emotions are in control and participants deal not with the issues, but instead attack each other personally."

There are two basic facts about couples who quarrel:

(1) They don't usually quarrel until after they are married.

This is because we are seldom honest before we are married. We are "playing roles" or on our best behavior. We couldn't stand to do anything that would jeopardize the relationship because we have a fear of losing that one around whom our world revolves. It's a similar situation when a husband and wife put their best feet forward for company. Their friends see them as loving, happily married, with no problems. Behind the closed doors of their home, however, they may scream, throw things, give the silent treatment or live in wretched boredom. When the doorbell rings, they put on their masks.

(2) Most fights are not fair; noone wins, both lose.

Since opposites attract, there is normally an anger-prone marriage partner and a fear-prone individual. One is more verbal than the other, and this is the one who can shout the loudest, argue the longest and just plain outlast the quieter mate. He or she has a distinct advantage when the fight begins and it doesn't take many months of marriage before he realizes it. Often, the quieter one gives in just to keep peace.

Coping With Contention

Is there any way of controlling quarrels? If a pattern has been established over a long period of time, it is going to be difficult—but it *is* possible—to control quarreling if both partners are willing to cooperate. The first requirement is to admit to each other that there are problems in the marriage and that quarreling is not the solution. Discuss the following ways to disagree in love and start NOW!

1. Make a commitment, together, to honesty and mutual respect. Read, in your Bible, Ephesians 5:21-33. Pick the right time to do this . . . when you are both feeling good, and are alone and unhurried.

2. Make sure your weapons, when you are upset with each other, are not deadly. No withholding of sex, manipulation, or tearing him down. God's way is to show kindness. Though you may be upset with the deed, don't hate the doer.

3. Agree *together* on the time for discussion. As your husband walks in the door from work, or as you face a huge stack of dishes, is the wrong time. If he wants to discuss it and you do not feel ready, be honest. Tell him, "Honey, can we talk about it later? I just don't feel emotionally up to it now." Don't, however, put if off indefinitely. The sore spot will only fester and cause a barrier for a longer time. Look for battle flags: when he becomes very quiet, bites his fingernails, swears in traffic, doesn't eat much. These all say, "There is a problem." Bring it up and encourage him to talk about it.

4. Be ready with a positive solution. Don't

just criticize without a better plan. Think of creative alternatives to what is bothering you. Ask God for wisdom, according to James 1:5, and pray that He will show you areas where you might be wrong. This is easier for God to do if you are having a daily devotion time. As you read God's Word, He will point out areas where you are falling down or need to mature. Invariably, when I feel I am right about something and am trying to talk my husband into changing his mind, God will speak to me through the Scriptures (and it will be a verse about submission to authority). I am grateful when He does this because I know that my husband is seeking God's will, and if I change his mind, we could easily get off on the wrong track. God doesn't tell him what to do through *me*. Although he listens to my counsel, the final decision is his.

5. Watch your words and guard your tone. The Bible says, "Don't use bad language. Say only what is good and helpful to those you are talking to, and what will give them a blessing" (Ephesians 4:29 TLB). When we speak softly and lovingly we are more likely to be listened to. If we have a condemning tone, no matter what our words say, we communicate our disgust. If one partner begins to be agitated, the other should pray for God to help him to speak in a loving manner so that the disturbed spouse will be more responsive.

6. Don't verbally "swing" at your mate in

public. Don't embarrass him by airing his faults to others or by cutting sarcasm. Many married couples disguise quarreling as kidding and do it in front of others because they are afraid to bring the matter up when they are alone. One woman we know always called her husband a "dolt" when the crowd got together. She said it kiddingly, but it was obvious from his reaction that he knew she meant it. My heart always ached for him and I was delighted when she became a Christian and stopped cutting him down.

7. When the discussion (or quarrel) is over, help clean up the mess. Be kind and gracious, tender and compassionate, and forgiving as you remember Christ's forgiveness to you. Quit when you are wrong, and surrender. Don't bear a grudge and be happy when it's over. A disagreement can be a fun thing when it's patched up—one of those "inside family jokes" that you laugh about for years.

The Family Joke

One of the biggest sources of amusement we've had in our married life is over a quarrel we had years ago. Our daughter was taking a course in counseling at a Christian college and brought home a personality aptitude test. It was one given to couples during premarital conseling to determine their compatibility. Each person was to rate himself and then his future mate on a series of questions. I thought it would be fun to take the test but happened, at the time, to be irritated with my husband over some small thing. I took a fiendish delight in marking him down in several areas where he normally would rate high. When he took the test, he looked at my rating of him and (since I hadn't discussed with him the matter that was bothering me) he believed that was really the way I saw him. You should have seen the way he rated me!! I have never been so thoroughly crushed, and I wondered how he could stay married to me if those were his true feelings. I barely spoke to him the rest of that day. At the end of the next day, he came home from work, got out the personality test, and tore it into little pieces. Then he looked at me and said, "I love you, and I apologize. And *that's* what I think of that test!" We asked each other's forgiveness and laughed all evening over the fact that we had taken a test to determine our compatibility after 25 happy years of marriage, and that it resulted in the worst quarrel we've ever had.

If you are prone to quarrel, ask God to take away your anger. Read the book of Proverbs and mark all the passages that deal with being angry. A fight in a marriage may release tension but the long-term wounds it inflicts are not worth it. We often say things we don't mean when we're angry. They are difficult to forget, especially for an introspective person, and he may carry them around for years.

When we were first married, whenever I

became angry with my husband, I would type a letter airing my grudges. I never gave him one of those letters. When I read them through afterward (and *always* be sure you do that) they would sound so ridiculous I would tear them up. It got everything off my chest with no harm done. Just don't leave one of them lying around where he might find it — tear it up and throw it away.

Agree to Disagree

Don't feel that you and your husband have to agree on every subject. It isn't necessary to always be trying to convert him to your way of thinking. Allow each other the freedom of your own opinions. The longer you live together, the more you will find that you become of one mind, but this is only possible when each of you stops trying to twist the other's arm to get him to change his mind. As you pray for objectivity and harmony, the Holy Spirit will unite your thinking and ideas so that there are fewer areas of dissention.

It is possible to be totally honest if it is done in love, but never wound your mate for the sake of tactless truth. Joyce Landorf, in her book, *Joyce, I Feel Like I Know You*, speaks of loving-honesty vs. atheistic-honesty. There is no love in atheistic honesty — it's the kind of bluntness that wounds people's spirits and hurts them for no good reason. Loving-honesty is a baring of feelings geared to draw people out and allow them to share their burdens. An example of atheistic-honesty would be as follows: When your husband, dressed for an important business meeting asks you, "How do I look?" and you reply, "Boy, you have really gained weight! I can remember when that suit used to fit you." What you've just done is shot his self-esteem full of holes, lowered his self-confidence 99 percent, and given him a large dose of inferiority feelings. He won't be at his best at the meeting no matter how well he has prepared.

Loving-honesty takes a different approach—it dwells on the positive. You would answer, even if he *had* gained weight: "Your hair looks especially nice, you look well-groomed and you smell terrific. I know your bosses will be impressed with how well you have prepared your report." You have complimented his good points, given him a feeling of confidence and zeroed his mind in on the most important aspect of his meeting.

This is what is meant by the well-known adage, "Behind every great man is a great woman." You can make or break your husband by your attitude toward him. A contented, happily married man shines like a beacon-light among his peers. Only you can make him that way.

11

What Makes a Marriage Good?

A leading pastor in our area recently remarked to a group of women, "There is nothing so comfortable as being with a relaxed woman who allows God to be in control." It occurred to me, as I pondered his statement, that "being comfortable" is very important to a man. I have often heard folks say, "I don't want to be rich—just comfortable." The dictionary defines *comfort* as "A state of ease and quiet enjoyment, free from worry, pain, etc." *Comfortable* is "easy, tranquil, undisturbed." It's a cheerful word, bringing to mind a crackling fire, popcorn, old clothes, a walk on the beach at twilight, good friends, an atmosphere of peace and congeniality. It means being relaxed and unpressured.

Comfort Begets Attention

Our husbands live in a dog-eat-dog world. We, if we do not work outside the home, have no conception of the competition, antagonism and frustration they must face each day in their jobs.

Rudeness, vulgarity and violence are often the rule rather than the exception. (Not that we don't experience kids quarreling at home, but it's not the same as when adults are out to step on each other in their battle for position and prestige.) When we consider this, it's easy to understand why our husbands need to be made more comfortable when they come home from work and not nagged, criticized and badgered.

We women, on the other hand, are not so concerned with comfort as we are with "attention." Wives often complain, "He doesn't pay any attention to me!" When they speak of wanting to be able to communicate with their husbands, this is essentially what they mean. *Attention* is defined as "thoughtful consideration, courtesy or devotion." Many a wealthy woman would trade, in an instant, her mansion, servants, designer clothes and social position for these. If we are communicating, we are getting our husband's attention. No one likes to be ignored, but when men are not comfortable in their homes, they respond by a lack of attention to us. Thus, the communication breakdown.

It seems, then, that our top priority should be to see that our mate is comfortable. If "comfort" to him means wearing an old pair of pants or holey bedroom slippers or some other outmoded outfit, it should be inconsequential to us. No prodding or hinting that his attire is not suitable or that he'd look better in something else. My husband has an old red plaid Pendleton shirt he wears when we are at our mountain cabin. While burning brush a couple of winters ago, a spark landed on his shirt and burned a hole in a prominent place on the back of it. That Christmas, I bought him a new Pendleton, and do you know where it has spent the past two years? Hanging in the closet while he wears the shirt with the hole in it. "It's so comfortable!" he says.

Comfort isn't necessarily sitting in an easy chair watching the world go by. Comfort can be working in the garden, fishing, stacking wood, playing tennis, sex—any activity (or *in*activity) where the heat is off and frustration, urgency and pressure are absent. Our husbands need this kind of atmosphere at home in order to live longer. If we add to the pressures they must withstand at their jobs, we either shorten their lives or cause them to withdraw from communication with us for self-protection. The comfort we provide for them results in the attention we want so much.

Flexibility Is Fantastic

There is even comfort in a small crisis if a man doesn't have a wife who falls apart at the slightest change or interruption of her plans. This is the kind of woman the pastor was talking about. She accepts these things as the norm, knowing that God is in control and her only responsibility is the right response.

Flexibility is a very desirable quality in a wife,

relative or friend. One husband said that the trait which irritated him most about his wife was her complete inflexibility. "Every time *anything* happens to upset her plans and threaten her getting her own way, she throws a tantrum!" he explained. "She either yells at me, runs into the bedroom and cries, or pouts for hours or even days afterward. She acts like a two-year-old instead of a 32-year-old!"

Did you ever have a friend who was so inflexible you hated to call and tell her you'd be a few minutes late picking her up for fear she'd be upset the whole afternoon?

People who always take offense and "never understand" are very hard on friendships and *impossible* in marriage. An inflexible spirit is a stumbling block to a man's comfort. It's extremely difficult to be relaxed and peaceful when his wife blows her stack at the least alteration of her plans. He would never dare to bring home unexpected company, invite friends over for a cup of coffee, surprise her with a weekend mini-vacation, make an unplanned purchase, or go on a spur of the moment picnic.

Everyone is inflexible up to a point, some simply carry it beyond the limits of good sense. According to Proverbs, "wisdom" is "having good sense." How can we tell if our flexibility crosses the boundary from the normal into the ridiculous? Following are some instances that fit into the "ridiculous" category.

- Our husbands suggest an after-dinner

movie or game of tennis and we refuse because it means having to leave the dinner dishes undone. The dishes can be done later, or in the morning. The joy of a night out together can never be recaptured.

• We refuse to try new products or inventions because "the old way is the best way." That dishwasher or microwave oven may save you hours of work and give you valuable time with your children or husband that you don't now have. The new laundry soap may be a definite improvement over what you've been using. The airplane trip may save you several days of driving and energy on your vacation and you may love flying, once you try it. Don't be "Sarah Stick-in-the-mud."

• We become angry when our vacation is suddenly changed, unexpected company drops in, or for some reason we can't wash on Monday. Life is full of surprises—and not always pleasant ones. A good preparation for ulcers, colitis or hypertension is to be rigid in our plans and bitter when we are unable to carry them out exactly as scheduled.

• We refuse to change our way of doing something, even though our way might be the hard way. My grandmother was of "the old school." That dear lady continued to use a knife long after potato peelers were invented. She cut away about 20 percent of the potato (including most of the vitamins) and occasionally a bit of finger, but she'd always used a knife and had no intention of changing. I enjoy reading "helpful household hints" and taking advantage of the shortcuts others have discovered in doing the old things a new way. Minutes saved in the execution of household chores means time to read a new book, to go for a pleasant walk, or to write that long-delayed letter to a friend. It is amazing to discover how we've become so set in our ways, when we make a concerted effort to change.

• The prospect of a new job or transfer, a move to another home or even a different area of service in our church threatens our well-being. Many companies transfer their employees. Homes are outgrown, or may become too large after the children leave. A man may have an opportunity to go into a different, more satisfying line of work. I would be the first to agree that moving is difficult. We moved four times in two years when my husband was with a large company. Our children were young at the time and the packing, house-hunting, changing schools and making new friends was traumatic, but the Lord never moved us anyplace that He didn't pave the way ahead. If you are in His will, He doesn't take anything away only to give you something worse—he gives you something *better!* There could be some risk involved in a change of employment, but don't stand in your husband's way if he desires this when the opportunity presents itself. Support him cheerfully and trust the Lord to take care of things.

Life is ever changing and God often moves us from one area of service to another in the church as we mature in Him and our usefulness grows. Just because you have "always" taught third grade Sunday School, doesn't mean that God wants you there forever. If the new superintendent replaces you with someone else, it doesn't mean the Lord is through with you. He has another, better job for you if your attitude is right and you seek His direction.

Resolve to Relax

Inflexibility is simply insisting on your own way no matter what the circumstances. It is the opposite of allowing God to be in control of our lives. Picture life as a movie with yourself as the main character. When you attend the cinema, you don't demand to write the story or plan the ending. You allow the author that privilege, and you relax and enjoy the sequence of events. You may cry when it's sad, become tense when it is frightening, and laugh when it is amusing; but you are interested to see how it all turns out and to uncover the meaning behind the story line. Life is the same way. It's so much better to allow the Author (God) to control the events of our lives and to relax and enjoy it. We can spoil life if we insist upon our own way, just as we would ruin the movie if we demanded that the actors ignore the script and do as we say. We would miss the meaning the author had in mind when he wrote it. I would certainly hate to miss God's purpose for my life.

Look at the long-range results of being rigid about our plans. Is it more important that the ironing be done at a certain time on a certain day or that we stop and take the time to go for a ride with our family in the country on a spring day? The fellowship and closeness of the time together is far more important than any schedule. If you find yourself to be inflexible, pray that God will help you to change. You will be happier and so will your family. Expect, however, to encounter many frustrating interruptions during your time of learning. It's the only way God can teach you to be flexible and to make your husband comfortable—to give you opportunities to be pliant and see the results. As the tension mounts, praise God for taking the time to save you from ulcers or a heart attack—and respond in the manner He would want. The peace and comfort of your home and the attention you receive from your husband will bless you far beyond any satisfaction you might have had at always doing every job on time and never changing anything!

12

Improving with Age

There's a popular saying that expresses the ideas that the only things which improve with age are wine and cheese. Many couples, particularly the wives, experience an adjustment problem when the last child leaves home. They may be in their early 40s, or in their middle 60s, depending upon how many children they reared and upon how late in life they had their children. Seeing children grow up and leave the home can be a traumatic experience and a time of boredom. There may be frustration, increasing loneliness, bitterness or neurotic behavior on the part of the wife. Of the marriages dissolved in today's courts, 40,000 a year are those of twenty years or longer. They've grown older but not better!

Not Ready To Retire

Unfortunately, as a parent, just when you get to be an expert at your job, you're retired! Mothers may find this time more difficult than fathers because Dad is still very active in his work when the children leave and, for him, the change is not so drastic. The house may seem a little more empty when he comes home, but his activities and hobbies go on. His mind is still geared to his job, and often to increasing responsibility in it. Mom, however, finds there is no longer any reason for her to be involved in many of her activities. P.T.A., Scouting, Four-H, etc., are not so interesting when her own children are not participating. The wash load has decreased, there is no need for her to do the baking and cooking on which she spent so much of her time, and the house remains clean, uncluttered and depressingly quiet! Her incentive for being home when school gets out has been removed, and if the children have moved to another city or state, she is even more lonely. No more long talks, shopping trips, or gang of kids cleaning out the refrigerator and leaving crumbs all over the furniture. Some women are unable to accept this, and go into deep depression. At the most potentially productive and carefree time of their lives, they clutch the past and refuse to open their hands to receive what God has for them in the present and future.

The Best Half

On the other side of the coin, there are many couples who find this to be the most delightful time of life. I was excited after reading a book by Ray and Ann Ortlund, entitled *The Best Half of*

Life, written specifically for couples in the middle years. The Ortlunds deal with making life from 35-50 and older the "best half." They speak of the sweeter companionship of these years, after the children have grown and left the nest. If we build our communication when we are younger, it is easier to make the transition to being a "single" couple again. Having just passed the 50-mark, and with all of our children a considerable distance away except for Gary — who is a senior in college — we can say that it really *is* the best half of life! We miss our children who are in other towns or states (and have the long distance phone bills to prove it), but God has given us so much to do that we can't sit around and be miserable. We have accepted the situation as from the Lord and are exploring new heights of marital happiness and service for Him!

One of the most delightful men I know is Tom Moore, the business manager at our church. He is a retired scouting executive and accepted the job at the church because he had always wanted to be in full-time Christian work. He has as much pep and bounce as any of the pastors with whom he works, most of whom are twenty to thirty years younger. His wife is assistant wedding consultant and keeps very busy with that. The Lord didn't file them away in a drawer when their family was grown and retirement came. God has given them an even more fascinating life, in a church of more than 4,500 people, because they were available. When you consider Corrie Ten Boom's life, you *know* the Lord doesn't have in mind for us to retire and vegetate. The so-called "twilight years" can be a blaze of glory if we are willing. God can even use senior citizens in poor health to minister to others through prayer and counseling. Their wisdom is invaluable to those who are younger and need help along the way.

What's the Next Stage?

Married life is said to have five stages, and understanding what is coming will help us to prepare for it. It really isn't necessary to plan in detail, when you are 25, what you must be doing at 55—God will take care of that because He has it all worked out, anyway. Our responsibility is to expect the changes to come and to be available to His plan for us. To some, retirement may mean lying on a chaise lounge on the deck of a cruise ship and being entirely free of obligations. That may be enjoyable for a couple of weeks occasionally, but I'm reminded of what our pastor, Marvin Rickard, always says: "I'd rather burn out then rust out!" (Sometimes he preaches as many as five sermons on Sundays, as we have six services. He's not getting rusty, that's for sure!) It is, however, up to the individual to gear his retirement activities to his particular needs, abilities and desires. We all need to feel useful and we can *be* useful when we give God the controls and step out in faith, expecting Him to make the best of whatever stage of life we are experiencing.

The five stages of married life are as follows:

1. Family Founding

From the wedding until the birth of the first child. This is the "getting to know you" stage. Often the husband and wife both work and sometimes the husband finishes college during this time. They are likely to live mostly for each other and have a small circle of friends they both enjoy. It is the "weaning away from parents" time.

2. Child Bearing

This stage covers the birth of the first child until the youngest starts school. This is the most demanding time on the mother and she seldom has any time to herself. The husband is usually just getting started on his career and may be working long hours.

3. Child Rearing

Kindergarten to beginning college or leaving home. Mother may have some free time to herself when the children are at school but these are very pressured years with many activities crowding the schedule. If you have more than one child, you will probably find yourself involved in several areas with a varied schedule.

4. Child Launching

From the first child's leaving home until the last departs. This stage normally contains quite a few emotional upheavals as the young people grow through different love affairs, broken engagements, successes and failures in school, important decisions to make such as life's work, life's partner, etc. The parent-child relationship undergoes a change with the cutting of the apron strings and the realization that they are now adults.

5. The Empty Nest
The parents are alone again. It is a crucial stage, depending upon how the communication between the couple has been in the years leading up to this point. Some may find they are strangers while others find it a time of real freedom.

Romance Is Right-On

If you find yourself, at any of the five stages, with communication and romance having slipped away because of busy hours spent making a home, tending to children and countless other activities, it's never too late to restore it! We need to constantly, each day, reaffirm and revitalize our love for each other. Think back to when you were dating your husband. Were there times when you sat in front of the fire and talked till 3:00 a.m., sharing your innermost thoughts and dreams? Do you recall spending so long in a restaurant booth, the waitress began pointedly refilling your water glasses and asking if you would like anything else? The time passed so quickly when you were together you didn't realize you'd been there for three hours. Then there was "our song," "our tree," "our bench in the park" and all those special, romantic places you went and things you did together. What happened to them after you were married? Those next stages of married life began bearing down upon you and the "romance" got lost in the shuffle.

In the case of most of us married couples, the day-to-day romance is too often relegated to last place on the priority list and we don't cultivate the habit of being romantic. Married romance isn't something we schedule once or twice a week and make a point to stop what we're doing and be romantic. It is an attitude of heart where we give each other a hug as we pass by—hold hands when we're shopping—whisper "sweet nothings" to each other, but *spontaneously*.

If it's been so long since you've done any of these romantic gestures, and you're afraid the shock will bring on a heart attack to your husband, start out slowly. Ask God to remind you to give him an extra hug once a day . . . or a pat on the head as you pass his chair . . . or squeeze his arm as you stand side by side examining the lawn for crabgrass. After the first week, ask God to nudge you more often until it becomes a habit to be romantic. If you really want to shock your husband out of his apathy, try whispering, "You're sexy!" into his ear as you stand in line in the checkout stand! It's so much easier to communicate with each other when you are demonstrating your love through action. We need to redevelop those attitudes of wanting to please our husbands, and regain the excitement we felt at being with him when we were first married. If you're reading this in disbelief and saying, "Oh boy! That's not possible at *my* age!" I can say with absolute assurance (because of having experienced it) that it is not only possible to have as good a relationship as you had then, but it can be so much *better* that you'll praise the Lord for it the rest of your days!

Cure For the "Empty Nest Blues"

If you are at the "empty nest" stage and feel life is pretty much over for you, there are some steps you can take to change things.

1. Renew your devotion to the Lord.

One of the most negative traits in a middle-aged to elderly person is that of self-pity. It adds years to our ages and alienates family and friends. Self-pity seems more prevalent in women than in men, and is a surefire method to keep people away from us, resulting in more loneliness and self-pity. I have counseled with many young women who consider it a boring duty to visit their mothers because of the constant complaints, detailed symptoms of illnesses (usually the doctors are unable to find anything wrong), and self-indulgent lives of the older women. They expect constant attention from their busy daughters, failing to realize that there are great demands upon their time in raising their familiies. If you find yourself irritated because your children do not visit you as often as you think they should, perhaps your devotional time with the Lord needs to be rejuvenated. He will fill those empty places in your life with Himself and service for Him, and time will begin to fly. Set your mind on things above (Colossians 3:2) and spend part of your extra time praying and reading. This will develop godliness in your life and your grown children will appreciate so much more their time with you. As you concentrate more on the Lord, you will find you do not need large portions of your children's time and will be content with whatever you have.

2. Receive your situation with thanks to the Lord.

Don't fight your situation. Recognize that if you are seeking God's will, you are right where He wants you to be. Adapt yourself willingly and rejoice daily. It's impossible to be depressed and praise the Lord at the same time. Read Ken Poure and Bob Phillip's little book entitled *Praise Is A Three-Letter Word"* (the word is "Joy"). Don't sit back and say, "I'm taking a vacation from Christian service now and someone else can do the work." This will lead to a boring, meaningless life.

Recently my husband and I were standing in line, waiting to go into church, when we noticed a rather bitter looking lady behind us. We introduced ourselves and asked her if she was a visitor. We were surprised to hear her reply that she had been a member for ten years, and we mentioned that it was unusual for us never to

have met before. "Well, I haven't been active,"
she said. "When I came here from my other
church I decided to take a vacation from church
work!" After ten years, she was still "vacation-
ing" and there was no joy in her face or voice.
That lady was sowing nothing; therefore, reap-
ing nothing.

3. Realize your promotion from the Lord.

We have been promoted from children to
mature adults and the blessings that go with it
are "exceeding, abundantly above all that we
could ask or think" (Ephesians 3:20). God will
open for us a ministry, if we're willing, that we
will never have to force, manipulate or design.
Through being available to teach a women's
Bible study, while in my 40s, God gave me a
ministry of writing books, putting on marriage
seminars and teaching classes on marriage and
family to young women. In the Bible, in Titus
2:3-5, we older women are told that this is God's
plan for us. Maybe you do not feel called to
teach, but you could care for the children of
these young women as they attend classes to
learn how to become better wives and mothers.
Telling Bible stories to, and caring for, their
little ones is every bit as important as min-
istering to their mothers. Sunday School teachers are always needed and workers in church
kitchens, making home visitations, hospital
calls, and taking meals to those with trials in
their homes, etc. are all areas where mature
women are able to serve. There are hospital
auxiliaries, helping in convalescent homes,

teaching craft classes, cake decorating, piano lessons, painting, cooking, helping in Christian Women's Club—hundreds of volunteer organizations which badly need help. No need for anyone to sit at home and feel depressed because "there's nothing to do." If you are friendly and willing, people will seek you out.

4. Replace your limitations through the Lord.

If you feel that your abilities are limited and would like to have a fuller, more joyful life, pray this prayer: "Father, change my abilities through your power!" After you pray that, watch out! God will surprise you beyond all expectations and give you ministries that will warm your heart, make you fulfilled and satisfy the loneliness you may feel. One of the most exciting concepts I've come across is that of the Christian's sense of destiny. Our heritage is higher than that of the non-Christian—for we have the power within us to achieve what would be impossible without it.

Much has been written pertaining to the discouragement felt by those people approaching middle age when they realize they've not attained the goals for which they had aimed. Many expressed deep disappointment in their lives and had very little hope that things would improve.

I first learned of the concept of having a sense of destiny when it was included in Pastor Paul Steele's "19 Principles for Training Children" (see chapter six). Then, one Sunday evening on the way home from church, I was thinking of it when suddenly it occurred to me that this heritage is not limited to any particular age group—it's for *all* Christians. As I considered the possibilities and scope of the idea, and realized this is our divine inheritance, it really blew my mind! I thought of Colonel Sanders and Corrie ten Boom, both pushing their centennial years, yet actively pursuing God's exciting plan for them. And I came to realize that middle age is no problem—God is in control of our destiny and we're not limited by our own puny talents and abilities! Life takes on a whole new dimension when you know who you are: a child of the King!

All of the attitudes and bad habits we have discussed in this book may have become so thoroughly ingrained in us that it's not easy to change them. Only with God's help can any permanent changes be made, and we need to remind ourselves each morning of the "3 P's." Begin the day with prayer, ask God to help you to be persistent in the attempt to change your attitudes, and to give you the patience to hang in there. Some days you may see great strides of progress while there are other times when you blow it. Your husband may respond quickly, or he may be suspicious and decide to wait and see how sincere you are—and whether your change in attitude is permanent. Expect setbacks, but do not be defeated by them. Keep your eyes on the positive signs, and trust God to do His work in your marriage.

COMMENTS, INSIGHTS

COMMENTS, INSIGHTS

Other Good Books
from Harvest House

☐ **WHAT KIDS KATCH FROM PARENTS.** This warmhearted mother-to-mother look at the role of motherhood and the enjoyable rigors of raising a family, shows that children can be trained "in the way they should go." Norma Steven tells of her feelings and experiences throughout twenty-two years of motherhood—of how kids KATCH more than they are taught. A delightful book for every parent. 0222—$1.60 (mass)

☐ **HOW TO ENRICH YOUR MARRIAGE.** Margaret Hardisty, author of the bestseller, **FOREVER MY LOVE,** is joined by her attorney-husband as they answer some of the hundreds of questions they have encountered in conducting seminars across the country. This book encourages an enriched marriage through proper use of one's channels of communication. 1385—$2.95 (paper)

☐ **HOW TO FEEL LIKE A SOMEBODY AGAIN.** Drawing on insights gained from his own personal struggle against feelings of worthlessness, Dale Galloway shares practical step-by-step principles to strengthen your feelings of self-worth. You, too, can break the bondage of a poor self-image, move ahead to new horizons and feel good about yourself! 130X—$2.95 (paper)

☐ **IN-LAWS, OUT LAWS.** You can enjoy your in-laws! In this book Norman Wright shows you how you can solve the most frequent in-law problems . . . ways you and your spouse can learn to accept each other's family and how you can help your in-laws understand and accept your life-style—how you can build positive relationships. 0796—$2.95 (paper)

☐ **HOMEMAKING,** An Invitation to Greatness, Norma Steven and Joyce Orwick. Recently a young mother of four wrote to Norma for help in her role as a homemaker. Through their letters Norma shares housekeeping hints, recipes and thoughts from the Word. It is the author's prayer that you will catch a glimpse of the homemaker's high calling and find your invitation to greatness. 1156—$2.95 (paper)

☐ **MIX BUTTER WITH LOVE.** A beautiful and practical cookbook written by Joyce Landorf—especially for her daughter-in-law. Inspirational—devotional—and full of delicious easy-to-prepare recipes for family and guests. A delightful gift for your daughter-in-law, your daughter or your special friend. Colorful, padded gift edition. Illustrated by famous artist, Francis Hook. 0354—$7.95 (gift edition)

☐ **HOW TO DEVELOP YOUR CHILD'S TEMPERAMENT.** Beverly LaHaye—pastor's wife, Family Life Seminar leader, author of the bestselling **SPIRIT-CONTROLLED WOMAN,** mother and grandmother—clearly presents ideas and concepts on how you can properly develop and train each of your children according to his or her temperament characteristics. 0346—$2.95 (paper)

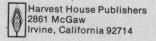
Harvest House Publishers
2861 McGaw
Irvine, California 92714